A Place of
Healing
for the Soul
☞ Patmos

A Place of
Healing
for the Soul
☙ Patmos

by Peter France

Atlantic Monthly Press / New York

Published simultaneously in Canada
Printed in the United States of America

FIRST EDITION

Library of Congress Cataloging-in-Publication Data
France, Peter.
   A place of healing for the soul : Patmos / by Peter France.
      p. cm.
   ISBN 0-87113-850-6
   1. France, Peter.   2. Orthodox Eastern converts—Greece—Patmos.   3. Orthodoxos
Ekklåsia tås Hellados—Greece—Patmos.   I. Title.
BX619.F73 A3 2002
281.9'49587—dc21   2001056596

Design by Laura Hammond Hough

Atlantic Monthly Press
841 Broadway
New York, NY 10003

02 03 04 05   10 9 8 7 6 5 4 3 2 1

☞ CONTENTS

⌒ INTROIT

"Spit on him," said the bishop. So I spat. A fine arc of spray fell gently into the shadow outside the church. I felt inadequate at not being able to muster a more emphatic spit, but it was only seven in the morning, I had missed breakfast and the target was not in sight.

We were standing by the west door of a tiny modern church in the suburbs of the port of Patmos. I could not face a ceremony at the ancient site in the harbor where St. John had baptized because the place was too public. But the news had got out and the good women who made up the congregation of St. Irene filled the nave and spilled out onto the forecourt. They were all looking at me. I felt slightly ridiculous standing there at the age of fifty-seven, barefoot and wearing only a shroud.

The shroud had given us problems. According to the traditions of the Orthodox Church, an adult convert is received into his new life wearing the garment he will have on when he quits it. But shrouds are not a stock item on the shelves of gents' outfitters in Greece; at least we could not find one on Patmos. And our inquiries raised a few eyebrows. So my wife had run up a simple white robe that stretched from neck to ankle out of a sheet.

I stared at the space in front of my feet and blinked to get rid of the colored disks that were spinning at the edges of my field of vision. It felt like the beginnings of a migraine brought on by tension, disturbed sleep and getting up at half past five. The nuns told me later it was the interference of Satan, who had just been expelled from my body by a triple exorcism:

> Fear, begone and depart from this creature and return not again, neither hide thyself in him, neither seek thou to meet him or to influence him either by night or by day; either in the morning or at noonday but depart hence to thine own Tartarus . . .

The dominion of Satan was in the west, the place of darkness. I had to speed him on his way there by spitting on him as he fled.

The bishop's hand on my shoulder turned me to face east, the source of light, to look into the nave. A forty-four-gallon oil drum stood in the center, two-thirds filled with water, fringed by a semicircle of monks. It had been painted on the outside with a metallic silver paint, which shone under the brilliant lights of electric candelabra. "Nobody who uses electricity believes in Satan;" the world of laptops and dental floss had no place for demons. A recent poll in Britain had shown that only 11 percent of the population accepted the existence of the devil—rather fewer than relied on horoscopes as a serious guide to the conduct of their lives. Was I about to join a credulous minority of cranks with a sentimental attachment to notions that had been abandoned by every sane person of my time?

I seemed to be standing outside time as I saw the dark beards and almond eyes of the monks echoed in icons around the walls. I felt the incense in my nostrils and saw a pious lady in black dip an elbow into the water and bustle out of the church and up the stairs to her kitchen, carrying a plastic jug. Then I heard the bishop, heavily bearded in Byzantine vestments of rich rose and gold brocade, whom I knew as a university don with a centrally heated house in north Oxford, pronounce in Greek the cleansing of the water.

The bishop turned to the deacon at his side, who was holding a small cup of olive oil. He leaned over and breathed on the oil and then, dipping his first two fingers in it, made the sign of the cross on my forehead, ears, chest, hands and feet. I was ready to be baptized.

That is to say, I had been made ready by the ceremonies of the Greek Orthodox Church for the sacrament, which gives entrance to the Church and to all the other sacraments. I was still a long way from ready inside. I was confused. I had always imagined that people presenting themselves for baptism had

Christ in their hearts and a bright glow of conviction in their eyes. I had seen that glow many times during the years I'd worked for BBC religious television. It proclaimed certainties which I had witnessed ruling people's lives. They worried me, since nothing in life deserves certainty, and unshakable convictions indicate minds incapable of change.

Fortunately for me the Orthodox Church accepts that nobody is ever completely ready for or worthy of a sacrament. The ceremony that was taking place was a help in getting there rather than a celebration of arrival: "Remove far from him his former delusion and fill him with the faith, hope, and love which are in Thee," said the bishop, placing his hand on my head. He led me to the metal drum, and I could see beads of oil floating on the surface of the water. There was a chair standing next to it, and I stepped up, climbed over the side and lowered myself into the water, which was waist-high. The bishop placed his hand on my head and pushed me under. Three times. In the name of the Father, the Son and the Holy Spirit.

The pious ladies with their plastic jugs had done a good job. The water was at blood temperature and I felt no shock, though the drum was a little cramped. I hoped the congregation would not think my gesture of pushing my thumbs into my ears showed I was unwilling to hear the message. As I had explained to the bishop, I had to keep the water out because I get ear infections and was not convinced that his exorcisms would expel bacteria.

Getting out of the drum was harder than getting in. The sides were high and the shroud was heavy with water. Clutching well-meaning hands at the elbows made me unstable, and I was eventually tipped out, dripping, onto the carpet. I had finally done it; or rather, it had finally been done to me. If ever baptism was going to work its magic, this one should. I was in the hands of a bishop and four priest-monks, the ceremonies had been meticulously performed and they were those of an ancient and unchanged Christian tradition.

And we were on the Holy Island of Patmos.

One

☞ A Place of Power

THE ISLAND OF PATMOS is a place of power. It changes people. They come here for a brief summer visit and find themselves returning, year after year, for the rest of their lives. If you ask them why, they all give the same answer: they are responding to a force which they can recognize but not explain. And which they find nowhere else.

Greek myth has an explanation: Patmos at the beginning of time lay undiscovered under the sea. The goddess Selene, the moon, who loved Artemis, daughter of Zeus, one night shone her rays through the water so that Artemis might see and fall in love with the island. She did, and asked her father Zeus to raise it to the surface. Helios, the sun, dried it off and made it ready for the first inhabitants. They were worshippers of Artemis and built her a temple on the summit of the hill overlooking the harbor. The island prospered under the care of Artemis, and a second temple was built to her twin brother, Apollo, near the harbor. There were games, a gymnasium and a guild of torch-bearers to celebrate the light of the moon. A further myth tells how Orestes, son of Agamemnon and Clytemnestra, fled to Patmos after he murdered his mother. He was pursued by the Furies and was protected from them by the power of Artemis. In the age of myth, Patmos was a place where the veil that separates the everyday from the eternal was thin. Some feel it remains so.

But the island was too remote to play a part in the earliest recorded Greek history. Although the fleets that attacked Troy must have assembled in nearby waters, Homer does not mention Patmos; and when the Athenians and Spartans were fighting each other or in league against the Persians, Patmos stood on the edge of the fields of conflict. Indeed, the only mention of Patmos in Thucydides emphasizes its remoteness. During the Peloponnesian War of 431–404 B.C., the Athenian admiral Paches heard that the Peloponnesian fleet, under Alcidas, had set sail from Ephesus to flee back home. "Paches, therefore, immediately set out in pursuit and went after them as far as the island of Patmos. From there he turned back again, since it appeared that Alcidas had got away out of reach."

Patmos was inadvertently put on the world map in the first century A.D. by a Roman emperor. The empire had been passing through a long period of relative calm. The last nine years of the emperor who died in 79 A.D. were called the peace of

Vespasian, and although it is possible that his son, Titus Flavius Domitianus, helped his elder brother to an early grave, he showed every sign of being a highly moral ruler in matters of public concern. He erected many temples and public buildings and investigated the probity of public figures, including the Vestal Virgins, three of whom he had buried alive for not coming up to scratch. He passed sumptuary laws regulating the amounts of money the rich could spend on themselves and issued edicts forbidding the overcultivation of vines and the neglect of corn planting. But the occupational hazard of the Roman emperors was always the possibility of assassination. This grew increasingly likely in Domitian's later years, as evidenced by the usual revolts in the army, and his attitude to the world moved from contentment to suspicion and on to paranoia. He seems to have been quite mad during the last three years of his reign, 93–96 A.D. He had himself proclaimed a god and took against any Christian in his empire who refused to worship him. In 95 A.D., he exiled to Patmos a Christian called John who had a vision in a cave there. The vision was recorded by John's disciple and became the most famous piece of apocalyptic writing in the world's literature. It is the last book in the Bible: the Book of Revelation, or Apocalypse.

    The story of St. John on Patmos is part of the island's mythology. To say that is not to dismiss it as untrue. From the Western perspective, myths are fairy tales: they may have entertainment value and even a moral message, but they are made up; they are fiction. If somebody asserts there is a historical reality at their center, we demand some sort of evidence before we can accept them as true. On Patmos, and perhaps in the wider context of Greece, there is a tendency to reverse this position: myths tend to be accepted in the absence of contrary evidence.

The exile of St. John to Patmos in the year 95 A.D. is not historically improbable. On the other hand, the account of his voyage, recorded by his disciple Prochoros, is seasoned with imagination. It is still told today. The boat on which the prisoners were sailing was caught in a storm, and one of the passengers was washed overboard. His anguished father was about to throw himself into the sea when John raised his manacled hands and made the sign of the cross. A great wave washed the man back onto the deck, and the storm calmed. The passengers and crew, including the ship's captain, were immediately converted to Christianity and delivered John to Laurentius, the Roman governor of Patmos, together with the story of the miracle he had performed. Laurentius freed John and arranged for him to stay at the house of Myron, his father-in-law. John exorcised a devil who had possessed Myron's son, and the whole family was converted. Myron's house then became the church from which John preached the gospel.

But there were priests of Apollo on the island whose authority was challenged by the new faith. So they climbed to a sulfurous cave at the summit of Mount Genoupas to ask the help of the evil magus Kynops in destroying John. The next day Kynops appeared in the harbor and dived into the sea to emerge with the effigy of a Patmian who had drowned. "Does anybody know this man?" he called to the crowd. "Yes," came the answer from a young fisherman. "He is my lost father." There was general awe and murmurs of admiration. Kynops challenged John to perform the same miracle. The apostle refused, claiming that his message was for the living and not the dead. The crowd saw this as an evasion, beat him and left him for dead.

But John recovered, and asked his small Christian household to pray with him for victory over Kynops. When the evil one heard that John was still alive, he swooped down from his mountain cave to the harbor and summoned a great crowd to witness the final humiliation of the apostle. Kynops leapt again into the sea and plunged to the bottom, at which point John made the sign of the cross and called on Christ's help. A whirlpool formed at the place where Kynops had dived, and the magician was turned into a rock on the bed of the sea. A buoy, noting a hazard to shipping, today marks this rock.

St. John converted the whole island, then went to live in a cave halfway up the mountain to meditate and pray. One Sunday in 95 A.D., he had a vision in which "one like the Son of man" appeared, surrounded by seven golden candlesticks, with eyes like flames of fire, a countenance like the sun and a voice like the sound of many waters. The voice told him to write what he saw to the seven churches in Asia. The visions were awesome: seven angels with seven plagues; four horsemen mounted on white, red, black and livid horses; a woman clothed with the sun; blood flowing from the wine press from the last days and the glories of the golden city, garnished with precious stones that await those who are saved. That book is the Revelation of St. John the Divine. It was written, according to verse 9 of the first chapter, on the island of Patmos:

I John, your brother, who share with you in Jesus
the tribulation and the kingdom and the patient endur-

ance, was on the island called Patmos on account of the
word of God and the testimony of Jesus.

Few travelers can have arrived on Patmos less susceptible
to the esoteric magnetism of the Book of Revelation than I, as I
stepped off the ferry for the first time in April 1987. For twelve
years I had been working as reporter for the BBC television
series *Everyman,* which explored religious issues around the
world. As is the way in television, we had been drawn to the
more eye-catching, extreme and deviant corners of our field of
interest, and I very soon noticed that almost every fanatical cult
we filmed justified itself by quoting the Book of Revelation. The
writing is so powerful and yet so obscure that it can be hauled
out in support of virtually any highly charged emotion. Along
with the rhymed quatrains of Nostradamus, it has become an
inexhaustible sourcebook of apocalyptic dottiness. I agreed with
the scholarly Dionysius, Bishop of Alexandria, who as early as
250 A.D. was plagued by ardent members of his flock who read
the imminence of the Second Coming into the Book of Revelation. He countered by pointing out that neither he nor they could
understand it.

The invitation to visit Patmos had come from a source
which made me hope the experience would be intriguing. Timo-
thy Ware, a childhood friend of my wife Felicia, had studied at
the monastery there after converting to Orthodoxy and had been
enrolled as a monk. He had risen to the rank of bishop, taking
the name Kallistos, and taught Byzantine studies at Oxford. I
had discussed religion with him and found him sympathetic,
openhearted, and highly intelligent (he fell asleep during his

final examinations at Oxford and still got a double first). He was spending a couple of weeks at the monastery and thought we might enjoy an introduction to the island.

Felicia, who had been baptized into Orthodoxy four years before, was delighted at the idea. She later admitted that a part of her enthusiasm sprang from the hope that if I had personal contact with Orthodoxy on a site so steeped in it, I might come to an understanding of the faith that was so important to her and which I had been unable to share.

My attitude toward religion was that of the great majority of people in the Western civilized world: one of sympathetic curiosity tinged with skepticism. I had always felt the aesthetic pull of Christianity when listening to a Bach chorale or the annual performance of *Messiah*. It had often seemed to me, however, that the impact of these works would be so much greater if the events they were celebrating had actually occurred—if the faith which inspired them were true and not an illusion. (I had been educated out of my Sunday-school faith at grammar school and confirmed in my unbelief by the prevailing mood at university.)

Social scientists had revealed the universality of the need societies feel to create and worship gods who manipulate those aspects of existence that are out of human control; depth psychology had revealed the unconscious mechanisms that promote feelings of dependency and a need for awe; higher criticism of the texts had destroyed forever the Bible's claim to infallibility. People who were, or wished to be thought, clever steered clear of religion.

All these were the intellectual reasons for rejecting Christianity. At a deeper and at the same time more immediate level, it did not appeal to me because religious people had always seemed, in the full flush of my youth, to lead diminished and colorless lives in the expectation of favors after death. Among the Methodists of my chapel-haunted childhood I had seen evidence of the world's growing gray from the breath of the pale Galilean, and I had rejected the promise of eternal bliss in favor of more present delights. I came to the decision, with the omniscience of an eighteen-year-old, that religion was a prop for the emotionally insecure and that it was unacceptable to the educated and intelligent.

But I came to discover as I developed as a freethinker that there was an eternal mystery about religion: so many people more intelligent and better educated than I seemed to accept it. I was constantly puzzled by the people I met who, even in private and with nothing to gain by it, would confess their acceptance of what seemed to me absurd. Also, I have to admit that, looking back on my life from the age of fifty-six, I seemed to have been more drawn to people with a spiritual dimension than to skeptics like myself. They had more weight, more substance. They were more emotionally generous and seemed to lack spite.

So, although I could not accept the claims of religion, I respected and liked religious people. I had lived among Hindus and Moslems in Fiji and studied their faiths. While there, I had depended on Catholic priests in remote stations for books and conversation. During the years I'd spent working in BBC religious television, investigating and reporting on different faiths, the stance I had to take professionally—that of impartial and uncommitted Inquirer—suited well my own position. So I arrived on Patmos having made a conscious commitment to give the island a chance but with no very lively hope that

anything it could do would change the often challenged but
secure agnosticism of forty years' standing.

The indignities and discomforts forced upon those who
choose to move from one part of the world to another by air have
changed the nature of traveling. The journey today is no longer
part of the holiday. Our first passage to Patmos was not relaxing.
"Package tours" are for the transport of packages, not of people.
Our aircraft had been modified so that the money lost by offering cheaper fares could be made up by carrying more passengers.
The seats were so jammed together that my knees lost circulation and every time the girl in front pressed her reclining button
my tray hit me in the stomach. The only way to release the pressure was to recline my own seat, which then struck the person
behind, and so on. As we tilted together toward the isles of
Greece, I reflected that this was the most uncomfortable journey
to the most unpromising location I had ever experienced.

Greece had always seemed to me to be rather oversold.
European civilization, we were always told, had its roots there.
But the aspects of that civilization which most obviously tried to
ape ancient Greece were to me the least attractive: neoclassicism,
balance, proportion, moderation. The appalling Greek motto
Moderation is best, so beloved of desiccated classics teachers,
seemed to me to preach a life lived about two degrees below
normal temperature. Moderation would come soon enough,
when age and infirmity made us incapable of enjoying life to
the fullest. To embrace it wantonly while still in full possession
of our faculties seemed a perversion.

I had another, more immediate reason for hesitation about
Greece as a place to spend a holiday: concern about the other

English people I could expect to find there. I didn't mind too much the exuberance of my fellow package passengers—all dead set on a couple of weeks of sunshine and booze, clearly sharing my view on the Greek motto. It was the prospect of running across associates from the BBC Arts Department that chilled the blood. I had put in a couple of years on a radio series called *Kaleidoscope* which concerned itself with music, books, theatre, painting, etc., during which time I encountered a subculture of tremulous aesthetes who all, it seemed, spent their spare time on remote Greek islands reading Proust. Patmos was, I had been told, remote and difficult of access, having no airport. It seemed all too likely that, after the long struggle to reach it, we would be greeted by a willowy figure in Paisley scarf and Panama hat waving a Gallimard paperback.

We flew from Gatwick to the island of Kos, home of Hippocrates, giant lettuce and package tours. From here we were to take a ferry north along the chain of Dodecanese islands to Patmos, arriving in the early evening in time to locate and settle into rooms let by a local householder named Maria Leosi. The arrangements had been made by Greek Sun, a travel agent with long experience on Patmos, whose tickets and itinerary I was clutching, together with a scrap of lined airmail paper on which was written:

> I asked one of the NUNS to inspect the room being offered to you in Chora, Patmos, by MARIA LEOSI. I have to tell you that NO SUCH PERSON EXISTS!!!!! You should ON NO ACCOUNT put ANY TRUST in this arrangement !!!

We had been getting letters from a newly acquired guide, Paula-Beryl, most mornings since we'd told her of our plan to visit Patmos. They were always on thin translucent paper and the text, written with black ballpoint pen, contained many exclamation points, capitalized emphases and heavily scored deletions. Over some of these she stuck white adhesive tape on which she wrote amendments. Most amendments were in the direction of intensification. Paula-Beryl lived life intensely.

She had seen a television program I wrote and presented some years before and had written to me about it. When I told her that my wife was Orthodox but that I was not, she took me on as a personal challenge and regularly sent me book lists and occasionally books she thought might be persuasive. She herself was born a Jew and had gone through a period of intellectual rationalism before converting to Anglicanism as an adult and then, after further study—she was a great student and had collected several degrees—to Orthodoxy. She had been baptized on Patmos and was an enthusiast for the spiritual qualities of the island.

When we had been invited to spend a couple of weeks there we had asked Greek Sun for a room in Chora, which we were told was a quiet village without hotels that surrounds the monastery. The agent booked us into a room "with balcony, kitchen and bathroom" in the aforementioned house. We told Paula-Beryl of this and she, anxious that the room should be entirely suitable, had telephoned a nun on Patmos and asked for a report on the place. The alarming response was capitalized in her letter.

The ferry was three hours late arriving in Kos. Nobody thought this odd. In fact, I was to discover that Greek people find our expectations of punctuality in public transport to be an obsessional neurosis. I once showed our local railway timetable to a Greek friend who collapsed with laughter when he saw that a train was scheduled to leave for London each day at 7:23 A.M.

As the ship plowed on through the darkness toward Patmos, we shivered on deck. We couldn't face the lounge because all Greeks of whatever sex and age seem to be chain-smokers and the television set in the corner, whose picture featured periodic hailstorms as we sailed between the island transmitters, blasted out sound at full volume. There was also, adding to the din, a clutch of portable radios pandering to that Greek fondness for noise which led the artist and writer Osbert Lancaster to say he knew he had arrived in Athens when he saw that the motorbike exhausts were fitted with amplifiers instead of mufflers.

We sailed into the harbor just after midnight and had our first experience of disembarking in Greece. This, like all Greek communal activities, is highly competitive. It has also become a ritual. Passengers on the ferry preparing to disembark form a phalanx—a Greek word describing a body of Macedonian infantry drawn up in close order—a dozen ranks deep. Behind them are heavy lorries, which start their engines and rev up for the disembarkation. Exhaust fumes mix with tobacco smoke and fill the hold. When the cranking of the winches begins and the tailgate starts to lower, the lights of the harbor appear at each side. Then the phalanx shoulders its baggage and surges forward in tight formation. Its members need to stay together because, as soon as the ramp clangs down on the concrete of the jetty, a boarding phalanx charges solidly up the slope in a desperate effort to get on the ship. Unless the disembarkers hold fast together, stragglers can be carried back into the hold with no further chance of getting off until the next stop, which is Piraeus.

We were jammed in row three and carried forward, past frustrated port police, peanut sellers and resolute ladies carrying signs reading "RUMS TO LET," to find ourselves dazed and grateful on Patmos soil. Immediately a cheerful, stocky man came up to us and handed over a plastic shopping bag. "Your breakfast," he said. "I'm Jannis Stratas and I booked your room. We'll get a taxi and Marouso will meet you up in Chora." "Marouso? I thought we were with Maria Leosi." "That's right. Marouso Kouva. The other's her maiden name. I expect it's still on the Greek Sun register. She's been with us for years."

So the infallible Paula-Beryl had slipped up. Or the good nun she had sent to inspect our room must have been from another island; otherwise she would have known the maiden names of the wives of Chora. At least, I reasoned, we should be out of reach of any of her promptings to piety in the rooms of the undiscovered Marouso Kouva, where we could luxuriate in the advertised pleasures of our own "balcony, kitchen and bathroom."

The taxi took the steep and twisting road in the blackness of the night as if it were on a trial run for Monte Carlo. At the time I thought we'd happened on a driver with an itch for speed, but when another taxi passed us on a blind corner at around sixty miles an hour I realized that the ferry had dumped a finite number of people at the harbor with a finite amount of money to spend, all wanting to make the ascent to Chora. So the more trips up and down a taxi could make, the more fares it collected. Reckless speed was financially prudent.

We could see nothing of Patmos but the lights of the harbor below and the departing ferry—it was amazing that the turnaround, involving passengers, cars and lorries getting off and on, took less than ten minutes. We arrived at a small square bordered on three sides by tall buildings and on the fourth by a low wall fronting a magnificent view of the harbor. A short, neat, bright-eyed woman with a ready smile opened the car door. "Marouso," she said. "Welcome to Patmos." We soon found out that, with these few words, she had almost exhausted her English vocabulary. But she led us, muttering and chuckling, through dark narrow streets for a quarter of a mile to her house.

The first disappointment was that the place was not a picturesque, traditional stone cottage but a modern construction in concrete blocks; the second was that it did indeed have a "balcony, kitchen and bathroom," but we had to share them with the occupants of two other rooms. There was another shock: propped against a jug of flowers on the table by our bed was a note from Paula-Beryl:

> WELCOME TO PATMOS. There will be a QUITE WONDERFUL liturgy at the women's monastery of Evangelismos tomorrow which I KNOW you WILL NOT WANT TO MISS!!! It starts at SEVEN A.M. Here are the directions . . .

We overslept; the liturgy and women's monastery would have to wait. We woke around eight-thirty and stepped out onto the balcony to face one of the great sights of Patmos. Across a broad valley, directly to the south, rose a mountain the shape a child draws when asked to draw a mountain: a jagged triangle, its outline broken by outcrops of rock with a few dark stone walls snaking among the scrub slopes and, at the peak, a tiny white cube of walls—the hermitage and church of the prophet Elias. A herd of about fifty goats was grazing on the slopes, the bells round their necks tolling with every movement and sending across the valley an irregular pulse of soft chimes that sounded like a distant peal of church bells underwater. Perched on a rock above them was a squat figure in a bright dress wearing a large circular straw hat.

This scene was bathed in what artists call "Greek light." To me, the impression was not so much that the quality of the light was different but that my eyesight had suddenly and dramatically improved. I could see the colors of the goats: mostly black and white or gunmetal gray, but in some cases a deep chestnut coat flecked with ash-blond hairs of an intensity I had never before experienced. The shadows among the rocks had a soft blackness and their outlines against the washed blue of the sky a sharpness and clarity that were breathtaking.

We sat at a small table on the balcony with bread, butter and honey to plan the days ahead. I felt glad to be there, at least in the sense that we had stopped traveling, though reserved in my enthusiasm for the place. Travel narrows the mind when time is short because we tend to see most readily what reinforces the ideas we arrive with.

The charms of Patmos, both Greek and Orthodox, were going to have an uphill struggle.

Two

☞ MONKS AND DANCERS

THERE WAS NO argument about the place to start. The Monastery of St. John Theologian on Patmos dominates the island. It is a massive stone fortress with heavy buttressing, protective towers and walls topped by crenellations. The only visible link with the church is a bell tower rearing above the north wall. Its origins are rooted in the turbulent years of eleventh-century Byzantium.

St. Christodoulos, the founder (after whom, it seems, half the babies on the island are still named), was, according to the traditions, a man of humble peasant stock who rose to be highly respected at the imperial court and the patriarchate. (He may in fact have been from a perfectly comfortable middle-class background, but tradition loves to root its saintly heroes in the soil.) Born in a village near Nicaea, in Bythnia, Asia Minor, he developed a teenage taste for the solitary life and became a hermit on Mount Olympus. He then traveled as far as Jerusalem and Rome before settling with the hermits in the deserts of Palestine.

There is a tradition in Orthodoxy that those who go off in search of wisdom in desert places should return to pass on whatever they have discovered to others. Christodoulos came back from Palestine and joined the monastery on Mount Latros, near Miletus, where he was made superior. The Turks were constantly raiding the area at the time and so he moved to the island of Kos and founded a monastery where he and a few followers could live in isolation. But Kos is a large island on the trade route along the Dodecanese, and the increasing population, together with regular raids from pirates, soon drove him to seek a quieter spot. He visited the island of Patmos, sacred to St. John and northernmost of the Dodecanese. He found it, to his delight, "totally deserted and fallen to waste, covered with brambles and thorny scrub, untrodden and so arid as to be completely barren and infertile." This was clearly a promising place for an ascetic foundation.

Christodoulos traveled to Constantinople to ask the emperor for permission to create what he called a "workshop of virtue" on the island. Alexius I Comnenus, who had first seen action against the Seljuk Turks at the age of fourteen and who never ceased to defend the empire against incursions, saw the value of monastic outposts at the edge of his world. He presided over a Christian empire and recognized that institutions which reinforced Christianity also bolstered loyalty to the emperor.

And Christian communities in the outer reaches of his lands might discourage the forays of the Turks. In the spring of 1087 the Pechenegs, a barbarian tribe that had troubled the northern boundary of the empire for two hundred years, sent in a huge army to invade. The region had few outposts and the invaders swept down on Constantinople. It took three years to defeat them.

The emperor granted Patmos to Christodoulos in the year 1088. The grant is recorded in an impressive chrysobull signed by Alexius in red cinnabar, which still hangs on the wall of the treasury of the monastery and which proclaims Christodoulos to be the island's "lord and master for all eternity and for as long as this world shall last." The imperial commissioner who surveyed the island and arranged its transfer to Christodoulos left us the first accurate description of Patmos.

> Having visited all parts of the island of Patmos, we found it deserted, uncultivated, completely covered with impenetrable thickets of brushwood and hawthorn, entirely arid as a consequence of the lack of water. In the whole island indeed we found no running water and no spring water, with the exception of a few small wells which rarely yield sufficient water . . . Moreover, what arable land there is is enclosed and as it were strangled by long chains of mountains. All the rest of the island is mountainous country, rough and unusable; in the arable part itself there are scarcely 160 measures capable of being ploughed; all the rest must be broken up with pickax and

mattock and watered by the blood and sweat of the farmer
... Of trees we saw not the slightest trace, apart from
about twenty desiccated pear trees.

Since the monks were clearly going to have a hard time sur-
viving off the land, the emperor allowed Christodoulos the free
use of a private ship for the monastery and exempted the island
from taxation forever. These last grants would enable Patmos
to become the leading maritime power in the region.

But, for Christodoulos, in the autumn of 1088 there were
only the hardships of a mountaintop site—he decided to build the
monastery on a hill overlooking the harbor, where a temple to
Artemis had stood—exposed to the biting north winds and rains
of approaching winter. He needed to build the monastery walls
as quickly as possible, "urged on by one thought, now," as he wrote
at the time: "the soonest to protect ourselves by raising them as
high as our strength allowed." Patmos, he quickly realized, was
prey to pirates, "and this is why Patmos is as it is, unpeopled, for
it has been raided by Arabs, corsairs, Turks, and always in danger of being taken captive."

The privileges granted to Christodoulos had made it possible for Patmos to develop as an independent monastic state,
rather like Mount Athos. Being a devout ascetic, he decided
that, like the Holy Mountain, it should be forever free from
the presence of women. A clause to that effect was included
in the chrysobull. The good monk was soon to discover that
his workmen had other views. For a time the walls ceased to
rise, until a compromise was found and women were allowed

to settle on the island with their children, so long as they stayed on a peninsula at the extreme north, to be visited by their menfolk only on weekends.

The building work was constantly in danger of interruption by raids from pirates, particularly during harvest time. Christodoulos gave instructions: "From the month of May onwards do not venture far, soldiers [he must have employed mercenaries] and villagers, but come and stay within the Monastery for protection; all must fill its bastions with stones and pay heed to everything, and fight courageously for the felicity of God and ourselves."

The church was completed in two years, but in 1091 the Turks attacked and the monks, "not having been convinced by works, gave way to fear and refused to stay on Patmos and departed." Christodoulos followed in 1092 and settled on the island of Euboea, where he died in 1093. The man he chose to be his successor as abbot declined, confessing later, "I did not want to go there . . . because Patmos was far away, the trip to reach the island was full of hardships, the danger from the Turkish warships and the pirates was great and also because the island itself was deserted and difficult to tread."

These testimonies about the dangerous condition of Patmos at the end of the eleventh century put in proper perspective the achievements of those monks who dared to return there and complete the building of one of the most sacred places in the Christian world.

Christodoulos was a scholar as well as a hermit, and he bequeathed his library to the monastery. He insisted that his successors on Patmos should not allow the books to be removed, and in his listing of the forms of manual labor permissible for the monks he made special mention of the copying of manuscripts. The ecclesiarch of the monastery—the monk appointed to supervise its ceremonies—was charged with the duty of looking after the books "with the greatest possible care." It serves us well, especially when we hear the claims made by the predatory traveling scholars of later years, to remember that the monastery was, from its foundation, a center of learning as well as a retreat for prayer.

WHEN WE LEFT MAROUSO'S HOUSE after breakfast, we followed the narrow street round the village of Chora to the monastery entrance. The high walls of houses and gardens on each side kept the street in shadow in the early morning. This brought another blessing to the village: the streets were too narrow for cars to pass between. For half an hour we lived in the dream that the only transport in Chora was the string of donkeys we saw collecting bags of rubbish. But then modernity struck and the first of the many scores of motorbikes appeared, carrying a man who had clearly been in better shape before the age of the Vespa.

As we walked up the slope to the monastery entrance, we had to pass a row of souvenir shops strategically placed to catch the eyes of passing pilgrims. These stores featured scores of tiny icons, brass bells, little plastic priests, photographs and guidebooks, video games and, at the bottom of the monastery steps, a miniature mechanical mandolin which was wound up by the shopkeeper so that the notes of "Never on Sunday" caught our ears as we approached, and rose pitilessly with us as we climbed.

The last stretch of broad stone steps has a metal handrail painted municipal brown on each side, and as we panted up we could make out a large painted notice by the outer door. It read:

YOU ARE IN A HOLY PLACE OF WORSHIP.
PROPER ATTITUDE AND DRESS ARE
THEREFORE REQUESTED.
THANK YOU.

And someone had added, written in ink on a white card: "NO SHORT."

It seemed to me a bit hard on the visitors here, the majority of whom were not pilgrims but lapsed-Christian tourists out on a treat in the Greek islands, to refuse them admission when they arrived dressed for holidays in the sun. But the monastery had been founded nine hundred years ago and clearly was in no hurry to bring itself up to date.

We passed through the massive outer doors and up a short flight of steps to the main entrance, which was guarded by twin towers with the usual slits for pouring down boiling oil. The final doors were much smaller—only about seven feet tall and six across—but they were made of timbers six inches thick, plated with metal. Beneath the embossed iron cross on the left-hand door was something like an enlarged cat flap, about two and a half feet by two feet, which opened independently when the main doors were barred. Through this it was possible to admit unidentified visitors, one by one, as long as they entered crawling on their knees.

Yet another flight of steps led to the inner courtyard of the monastery, where we saw a notice board at the entrance on which, over the years, visiting linguists had penned:

NE

LES PANTALONS COURTS /SONT PAS

PERMIS

KURZE HOSEN SIND NICHT ER LAUBT

SE PROHIBE LA ENTRADA A ESTE

MONASTERIO EN SHORTS GRACIAS

NO SHORTS. PANTS.

But the monks had compassion for those who'd been reared with the relaxations of modernity. Just beneath the notice board was a heap of clothes of various girths and lengths for the use of those offending the battery of regulations: jeans, flannels, gray-and-white striped jailbird trousers, pajama bottoms and a wide selection of brightly colored cloths, all there to conceal offending knees.

The walls and ceiling of the exonarthex, the outer western porch of the church, where catechumens, penitents and women once sat, were covered with flaking wall paintings which told the story of St. John's first visit to Patmos. Inside, in the narthex, to the right of the main entrance to the nave is a large twelfth-century icon of St. John in a massive, ornate silver frame. The image was a shock to me, because I had thought of St. John as the youngest of the apostles; the one who lay casually on Jesus' breast at the Last Supper; the disciple whom Jesus loved; the one who with the vigor of youth had outstripped Peter when running to the empty tomb. And here was an old man with lined face and bulging forehead, eyes turned inward or toward something beyond, holding, but not looking at or showing, a book with the first words of his gospel: Eν αρχη ην ο λογος—"In the beginning was the Word."

Inside the nave, the main impression is one of dim yet lustrous opulence. The space is small, but ornate silver lamps crowd together above your head, a large brass candelabra featuring twenty-five candles hangs in front of the iconostasis—the icon screen that separates the sanctuary from the nave—and eight oil lamps in filigree silver add still more light. The iconostasis, which seems to lean threateningly over the nave, being too large and heavy for the space it dominates, is covered with elaborate wooden carving that is in turn covered with gold leaf. On the right of the iconostasis is another icon of St. John—Russian, from the late seventeenth century—in which he is again portrayed as an old man but a few years younger than the one in the narthex, with balding head and thick gray curls. This St. John looks straight at you, holds his book for your edification and points with quill pen to the opening words.

It was a relief to step from the dark and claustrophobic atmosphere of the main church into the light and peace of the Chapel of the Virgin next door. This is even smaller—only eight and a half meters by three meters—with a vaulted roof and marble floor. Around the walls are dark seats with high armrests polished to near whiteness over centuries of rubbing by hundreds of monkish forearms during thousands of hours of services. The walls have stark paintings in glowing colors of faces of Byzantine saints gazing impassively into space. These are not the highly spiritualized figures of icons but portraits of real people, like those who come here from local villages or other Greek islands to gaze up at them. On that first visit the chapel seemed filled with an audible silence, with an atmosphere in which I could feel a pressure on the eardrums but could detect no sound. There was a sensation of the numinous, a presence which even I felt as a prompting to awe.

As we entered, Felicia had crossed herself and kissed the icons on the iconostasis. This was, for her, and for the hundreds of thousands of Orthodox pilgrims who came to this place, the natural response to its sanctity. I felt excluded by my inability to follow the ritual, but knew that it would have been dishonest to try. I remembered how, for fifteen years as a district officer in the Fiji Islands, I had been welcomed on tour by traditional ceremonies in which I was presented with a sacred whale's tooth. I had learned that, on receiving the tooth, I should hold it up and say a formula of words that constituted a prayer to the gods: "I receive this tooth that your lands may prosper." Nobody thought it dishonest of me to utter this prayer to gods I did not believe in. And yet I would have found it shocking, as an unbeliever, to go through the pious gestures of a Christian in a Christian holy place. Agnostics can be punctilious about religious ceremony.

That evening we had our first experience of dining out on Patmos. We followed the signs reading "CENTRIC SQARE" to get to the heart of Chora and found a small open space with narrow streets feeding into it from each corner. On two sides of the square were cafés, each with a few tables inside and many more filling the paved space outside. The tablecloths at Vangelis

Restaurant had red checks; those at Olympia were blue. We chose Vangelis, as it seemed more active, though at 7:30 P.M., which was to us a reasonable time to start on an evening meal, there were few other customers. Vangelis, slim, swarthy, pencil behind the ear, mustache, broad grin, greeted us: "Welcome. You like to see my kitchen?" And we went inside to a small back room in which ranged on a table were large pans of green string beans stewed with olive oil, tomatoes and onions, stuffed vine leaves, giant haricot beans in tomato sauce, mounds of spaghetti gleaming with oil, trays of meatballs, stuffed tomatoes, stuffed green, yellow and red peppers, macaroni cheese, moussaka, pasticcio and a rack of whole chickens slowly turning and dripping on an electric spit. Vangelis announced each dish with the relish of somebody seeing it for the first time and then led us out to a table on which he placed a small basket of bread and cutlery, two full glasses of water—together with, oddly, two half-empty ones—and a menu. Then he took the pencil from behind his ear and stood, head to one side.

We were dazed at the sight of so much food. To select dishes by name from the printed page of a menu invites cool analysis and comparisons on the basis of experience; to be confronted by the sight and smells of great quantities of exotic and succulent dishes crammed together in a small space is baffling. "How about a few starters?" I asked, playing for time. Vangelis grinned and took a deep breath. "I have tzatzikitaramasalata gigantesbeetrootwithgarlicsaucegreeksaladtomatosaladtunasalad melitzanosalatakolokithakiakalamari—" he began. "We'll try the first five," I interrupted, and tossed back one of the half-empty glasses.

From the next-to-last pressing of the grape skins and seeds the Greeks produce a fiery distillation which often touches 90 percent proof. It is colorless until mixed with water, when it turns milky. Warmhearted restaurateurs often hand it out on the house to customers who are actual or potential regulars. This is ouzo. It sat unsuspected in my half-empty glass. Nothing in my experience in the field of strong drink, which is extensive if unsophisticated, gets so rapidly to the centers of sobriety and dissolves them so immediately and totally as ouzo. The process of intoxication from beer or wine or gin or whiskey is gradual: first there's the feeling of warmth and amicability, then the relaxation of inhibitions, then the inflow of insights into the human condition as the terminal consonants become difficult to manage, and so on. With ouzo it all happens at once, espe-cially to the absolute beginner. I caught my breath, wiped my eyes and patted Felicia's arm to reassure her that I was not hav-ing a fit. Speech returned sometime later.

The first four starters arrived. *Tzatziki,* a dip of grated cucumber, yogurt, olive oil and mashed raw garlic, cleared the sinuses immediately and readied them for the smoky pungency of the *taramasalata*—pink fish roe pureed with potatoes. The *gigantes* were giant-sized haricot beans in a delicious fresh to-mato sauce, and the sliced beetroot was served with a placid-looking off-white sauce, which turned out to be a high-octane blend of raw garlic, olive oil and bread crumbs. True Greek salad has no lettuce, and we were served a large bowl of chopped tomatoes and cucumbers dressed in olive oil and scattered with raw onion and olives, then topped by feta cheese. Five plates were put in the middle of the table, and we helped ourselves.

As we began to eat I caught sight of someone waving from inside the café. Sitting at a table with three other men was Theologos, husband of Marouso, our hostess. They had been drinking coffee but had moved on to ouzo, as I could tell by their milky glasses, which they sipped with a mixture of relish and caution. Theologos was a warm, extroverted enthusiast with a deep laugh that topped the conversation and echoed around the square. "*Kali orexi!*" he called—"Good appetite!"—and, pointing at our table with its five plates laden with food, he gave a thumbs-up sign and shouted, "*Pan metron ariston!*"

The words "*Pan metron ariston*" ("Moderation is best") were said to have been inscribed on the walls of the temple of Apollo at Delphi. They were the leitmotif of classical studies as taught in England. I have mentioned the hostility I always felt toward this philosophy. Because of its association with the classics, I formed the impression that Greeks were all like the teachers of Greek: middle-aged, balanced, careful people who always got up from the table feeling slightly hungry. I was so bothered by this that I had mentioned the words to Theologos that afternoon to get his reaction. What did he think of "*Pan metron ariston*" as a guide to the good life? He spoke very little English but left me in no doubt, by the enthusiastic nodding of his head and the thumbs-up sign, that he knew and indeed lived by the motto.

Vangelis arrived carrying a liter jug of wine, which we had not ordered, and two glasses. He nodded toward Theologos, who laughed and raised his glass to us. "*Pan metron ariston!*" he shouted, draining it. I was to discover that Theologos toasted moderation every night—enthusiastically and extravagantly.

Greeks don't go out to eat until most of Northern Europe is tucked up in bed. By around ten o'clock, families were arriving from all four streets and pushing tables together so they could have dinner with friends. Children of all ages were chasing cats around the square and being called back to tables piled high with food. Inside the café the jukebox was playing passionate Greek music and three old men danced in a grizzled circle, connected by the handkerchiefs they jointly held, their movements fluid and controlled, as if they, and not the music, were in charge. Their heads were thrown back and half-smiles lit their faces, as if they knew all about passion, had felt it and could feel it again. They were dancing for themselves and not for the people watching, but they were applauded and cheered when the record came to an end.

I realized something important: the people applauding were their friends and relations. This was not a show put on for the tourists but the way life was lived on the island before the tourists found it. And the most striking thing about their approach to life was its intensity, its urgency. These were not analytical, reflective people. The balance, proportion, seemliness and moderation of classical Greece were nowhere in evidence. What was clear was the overwhelming importance to them of the immediate experience. Their lives were being lived fully in the present. *Now* was what mattered. The grandmother scooping up a running child to squeeze and kiss; the bald man bending over the plate of pasta, the veins across his head throbbing with pleasure; the plump mums shouting "*E viva!*" to each other as they raised and drained their glasses; the young men screaming homicidally in the corner as they conducted what in the rest

of the world probably would have been a rather polite inter-
change of views on current events; the old men resting from their
dance but watching it all intensely. Even to them, *now* was what
mattered. Not the past, not the future, but the actively experienced present. *Now* is when time intersects with eternity.

We had moved on from the starters to the main course—
Felicia was tackling half a spit-grilled chicken as I weighed into
three chunks of stewed lamb the size of cricket balls—when I
saw an unsteady figure pushing his way through the tables toward us. Theologos gave a shout of delight as he waved a hand
at our table, which was stacked with half-empty plates and wine-
glasses. "*Pan metron ariston!*" he called over his shoulder as he
tottered off into the night.

So the Greeks on Patmos, it was turning out, were not
hung up on moderation. And I had the feeling that I had come
across their zest for living before, in another place. It had nothing to do with their living on an idyllic and sun-soaked island:
Fiji had plenty of those but no sense of urgency. Then I remembered that ten years earlier I had done a film about the Russian
Orthodox Church in London. These Russian Christians, I discovered, seemed to turn English Christianity on its head. In
England, Christians are expected to be sober citizens who conduct themselves according to middle-class proprieties—the very
definition of the word "Christian" in the *Oxford English Dictionary* is that of a "decent, respectable or presentable person."
But these Russians ate and drank hugely and would burst into
song and roar with laughter all night, given half a chance. They
shouted and wept and kissed each other, all of which I took to
be Russian characteristics overwhelming basic Christian civili-

ties. But when I discussed it with them they would have none of that. God had become incarnate, they claimed, so matter could be spirit-bearing and we had a duty to celebrate fleshly things. "We are an incarnational faith!" they would cry, uncorking a second bottle. "We are a trinitarian faith!" they would shout, uncorking a third.

So the similarity of behavior between the great continental masses of Russia and this tiny island population in the eastern Mediterranean was, perhaps, explained by a common faith, that of the Orthodox Church. It was clearly worth looking into.

Three

☞ NUNS AND REAL ESTATE

WE ARRIVED BACK at our rooms at one of those hours between midnight and dawn to find a six-page scribbled note in a familiar hand, urging us not to miss the morning service at the Convent of Evangelismos:

> Would Felicia be prepared to wear dresses of THIS TYPE [a sketch of a long-sleeved, high-fronted dress]— i.e. without very much BARE ARM and looking "Womanly" and NON-MALE? BY TRADITION the islanders THINK that if a woman IS religious and SEEMLY she will not wear SLACKS or walk about in brazen SEMI NUDITY.

There followed four pages of minute directions on how to find the convent and a recommendation that we get there no later than 6:30 A.M. After a brief nap, we struggled out of bed and made our way drowsily through the narrow streets out of Chora and then down a long cobbled donkey track leading west toward what looked at a distance like a granite castle with huge, square, crenellated towers. About four hundred years ago there was a hermitage on this site overlooking the Icarian Sea. It was called the Hermitage of Evangelismos. The word *"evangelismos,"* meaning "glad tidings," is used for the Annunciation which Gabriel made to the Virgin Mary of the coming birth of Christ.

At that time, the beginning of the seventeenth century, the abbot of the Monastery of St. John was a famous scholar from Crete named Nikiphoros Chartophylax. He had tried to re-kindle an interest in Greek culture during the dark years of Turkish domination by founding a school at the monastery where pupils were taught Greek, Latin, philosophy and theology. It was very successful and the forerunner of the Patmian School, of which we shall hear more.

In 1613, Nikiphoros fell ill with the plague and went down to the Hermitage of Evangelismos to isolate himself from the monks and wait for recovery or death. He prayed to St. Luke, the physician, and was miraculously cured. In gratitude he built the Chapel of St. Luke and installed there an iconostasis from Crete, which was faced in gold and hung with Cretan icons.

For the next three hundred years the hermitage was occupied by holy men in search of solitude, but in 1937 a remarkable man founded the Convent of Evangelismos there. He too had a mission to revive traditional culture. He was Amphilochios

Makris, abbot of the monastery and thorn in the side of the Italian occupiers of Patmos. During the Italian occupation, which lasted from 1912 to 1948, Patmians were forced to learn Italian at school, were forbidden to teach Greek and were discouraged from practicing their Orthodox faith. Some of the older Patmians still talk of the times when they were governed by a people they disliked but learned to get along with. They used to run away from school because they did not want to learn Italian, but then their parents were punished so they went back. They always spoke Greek at home and whenever they were together in the streets, but switched to Italian if any Italian came within hearing distance. At school, they say, Roman Catholic priests would occasionally try to persuade them to convert to the pope, but nobody took them seriously and the Italians basically followed the example of the Turks by allowing them their Orthodox liturgies.

In opposition to the attempts to turn Patmos into a little piece of Italy, Father Amphilochios arranged for Greek lessons to be given at the monastery and encouraged the parish priests to keep up the traditional liturgical calendar throughout the year. The Italians, for this and other seditious activities of its kind, exiled him for a time.

But on his return to Patmos he founded the Convent of Evangelismos. There women could live according to the ideals of the early Christian monastics. They could follow the teachings of the fathers of the church, could revive the traditional Byzantine chant and the moribund ecclesiastical style of embroidery and could run secret schools where the children of Patmos might learn their own language and traditions. He also encouraged the nuns to care for their gardens. Father Amphilochios had a particular enthusiasm for trees. He used to say that anybody who loved life must love trees, and vice versa. On sinners who came to him for confession, he would impose the penance of planting a tree and watering it for three years. So fruitful was this corrective regime that the steep western slopes of the valley that runs from the convent down to the sea are now dense with trees, each commemorating a Patmian peccadillo.

As we approached from the east side we came to an outer gate in a low wall that surrounds the grounds. A small handwritten sign warned that the convent was open only between the hours of 9 A.M. to 11 A.M. and that "Women in undecent dress (trousers)" would not be admitted. On the left-hand side of the short drive that leads to an inner gate we saw a scrupulously kept vineyard with trees planted in regimented lines, carefully pruned, each one with a stem whitewashed against insects and each row sheltered from the birds by long nets—the first evidence of a disciplined life. I found it slightly unsettling, given the informality veering into recklessness that seemed to characterize life elsewhere on Patmos. Furtively, I checked my dress.

The inner gate led into a sheltered and ordered garden with simple wooden seats and tables grouped under the trees, potted plants that were shining and well watered and a drinking-water fountain, all spotlessly clean. A stone-flagged path led to the front door, over which was a mosaic showing the Archangel Gabriel kneeling in front of a seated Virgin Mary with the word "*evangelismos*" underneath. The door was heavy and well supplied with bars but slightly open, so we went in, to find a tiny office on the right-hand side, with a table, chair and telephone, and steps leading down. We took the steps and found an ancient tower on the right with an aperture for pouring boiling oil on pirates, which I recognized as part of the original hermitage, and to the left across a courtyard the Church of Evangelismos. There were rows of chairs outside the church, presumably for an overflow of congregation. It became clear why they might be necessary when we went in.

From the entrance door at the west end to the iconostasis cannot have been more than ten paces, and across the nave perhaps four. Along the walls were stalls with high armrests for standing occupants. But there were only five spaces on the left and four on the right—the extra space being taken up by the bishop's ornately carved wooden throne and the steps leading up to it. Since only a bishop could occupy this throne, the provision of stalls for non-Episcopal members of the congregation was restricted to nine. And it seemed that these nine places were all for men. Two were occupied. The women were sitting in rows of chairs at the west end of the nave and spilling out into a side chapel.

Even half-empty, as it was when we arrived at 6:30 A.M., the church felt crowded. Every square inch of roof and wall space held paintings of saints or scenes from the life of Christ. I remembered reading that the Orthodox faithful do not need to be literate because they can hear the words of the gospel and see them interpreted in paintings every time they go to church. Being unsure where I should go, I took the stall farthest from the seated women and closest to the iconostasis.

A choir was singing softly on a raised platform at the west end of the church. This was striking, both because the voices were female and because they were subdued. I had heard only the usual male cantors in Greek churches, who tend to vocalize in a metallic, strangulated wail, as if, somebody once said, God is deaf. These nuns seemed to be singing to somebody close by. The hymns contain the entire theological teaching of the Orthodox Church, so that a worshipper has only to listen to them to receive the full doctrine of the faith. Singing is not an optional extra: it is worship itself.

Standing apart at the front of the church, I had the strong feeling that all my senses were under assault. Music filled the dark interior, and in the flames of the candles colors glowed from all around, along the walls and over the ceiling. The air was heavy with incense, and where I stood a rich sweet fragrance rose from two gardenia blossoms floating in bowls of water at the base of an icon. It seemed to me the most magnificent theater; but then, I thought as an observer, the Orthodox Church had had two thousand years to develop its histrionic techniques.

The service lasted almost two hours. Anthony Bloom, the most charismatic of Orthodox apologists in Britain, once advised someone seeking for the truth in Orthodoxy to forget books and simply attend a liturgy. "The service is long," he had warned, "but even Orthodox services eventually come to an end. And if you simply stand there and are open to whatever happens, something might." I stood the whole time: I did not know when sitting was allowed, and as I'd stupidly put myself in a spot where the congregation was behind me, I couldn't watch them and copy. I tried to stay open to "whatever happens," but after an hour or so my knees were getting stiff and I was becoming irritated by all the repetition. I came out feeling that I had had an intense—if overlong—aesthetic, but not spiritual, experience.

After the service we were all led into a reception hall, spanned by two elaborately decorated arches, with paintings of saints and imposing photographs of Patmos church dignitaries in full regalia on the walls. Along each of these walls were heavily carved dark wooden chairs; in addition, there were three or four more opulent ones decorated with gold and upholstered in burgundy satin. The latter were not reserved for distinguished guests, it seemed, since I was ushered into one of them. Then in came three sisters, each bearing a tray. The first had tiny white cups of strong black Greek coffee, the second a basket of baked sweets and the third row upon row of liqueur glasses filled with a promising clear amber fluid which turned out to be cherry brandy.

It was when the brandy-bearing nun bore down on me for the third time that I had my first revelation. Until then my reactions to the convent had been what I took to be normal for a nonreligious intruder: the unfamiliar rites made me feel out of place; the ordered formality of the surroundings made me stiff and awkward. And I felt, above all, the great sadness of seeing so many women of all ages—many of whom were young and in another context might have been thought attractive—so withdrawn, their white, severe faces half-hidden by cowls, the humanity sucked out of them by the severities of their asceticism. Then the cherry-brandy nun looked straight into my eyes, shook the tray a little to encourage me to another glass and smiled. I realized that here was a young girl who was bright, warm, enthusiastic and glad to be what she was. The withdrawal that I had noticed, the practice of walking with eyes lowered and faces half-hidden, was a practical way of getting around undistracted.

Unlike politicians, nuns have no need to be noticed or to notice. But when called on, when confronted by a person, they respond immediately, directly and totally.

Most of the nuns spoke only Greek. We sipped our coffees and watched them busily carrying trays around the reception room. They were entirely focused on what they were doing, with a concentration that seemed to cut them off from their surroundings. But if somebody spoke to one of them, her face would light up in a smile and she would focus just as completely on the person.

I realized that this is the essence of humility. There was a complete absence of regard for the self in the way they lived. Either the work mattered or the person mattered. I had thought humility meant accepting that you did not amount to much, that you should always devalue yourself or your achievements when talking to other people. I had been influenced by the ethos of New College, at Oxford University, the essence of which is that you must never make your superiority to others apparent to them. This was essentially the English form of humility, which built the empire and realized, for a time, the prophecy that the meek would inherit the earth. But it was cant. Real humility, I learned from the nuns of Evangelismos, is not thinking yourself less than the dust. It is thinking of others so completely that you do not think about yourself at all.

Most of the older sisters were tiny, their average height about five feet and so frail you felt that a strong breeze would carry them away. As we were about to leave, one of them, who seemed even smaller than the rest, detached herself from a group and came toward us. She had a pale, lined face and thin, fragile-looking hands—the only parts of her that were visible—but her eyes were bright and lively and her mouth was smiling. She introduced herself as Sister Paraskevi, which curiously meant to us Sister Friday, though we later learned that Paraskevi means literally "preparation" (Friday being the day of preparation for the Sabbath). There is, in the Orthodox calendar, a St. Paraskevi after whom she took her name. She had the duty of looking after visitors and was chosen for this role at least in part because she spoke both French and English.

Sister Paraskevi, who was to become our closest friend at the convent, was an unlikely combination of the spiritually austere and the pragmatic. She had worked in a bank as a young woman and brushed hard against Mammon and his devotees before hearing the call to a life of prayer. From the moment we met her she seemed to feel that we were the most important people in her life. We later discovered that a large group of people all over the world had that same feeling of special intimacy with her. This was her brand of humility. It seemed to me that she embraced Felicia as a fellow Christian and saw me as an urgent challenge. I was an unbeliever and therefore in some danger of perishing everlastingly, but perhaps of more immediate relevance, I was missing the whole point of the here and now. Sister Paraskevi not only took on personal responsibility for our spiritual progress within a couple of days of having met us; she also appointed herself our estate agent.

Felicia had decided that we had to have a house, for within forty-eight hours of arriving on Patmos Felicia and I had agreed that we wanted to experience more of the island. Charming though our location in the rooms of Marouso was, we were both keen to find a place where we could have a kitchen, a bathroom and perhaps even a veranda to ourselves. No such accommodation seemed to exist in Chora. We asked about renting a house and discovered that they were available but cripplingly expensive. We looked over one that had a couple of bedrooms and a charming view of the harbor, but the rent was three million drachmas for the summer season. As we could raise only a total of six million, this would vanish in a couple of summers, with nothing to show for it. We had, at the time, no firm plans to spend long periods on Patmos but felt in an unfocused way that if we could buy a cheap hovel we would feel closer to the place. And Felicia's instinct for nest building has always been resolute. So we set off house hunting.

The prospects were challenging to Felicia, alarming to me. The charms of Chora had been discovered by a well-heeled international group, which had bought up the larger houses and occupied them for a few weeks each summer, while usually renting whatever other accommodations were available for their guests. So houses in Chora were at a premium and their prices were on a par with those of central London. Furthermore, most of the houses on Patmos were owned by families, and the families of Patmians tended to be far-flung. Even if we found a place we liked and could manage to agree on a price, the deal would then have to be discussed with brothers and sisters, cousins and possibly nephews in Houston, Frankfurt, Birmingham or Melbourne. The chances of getting general consensus were slight.

Finally, to cap it all, Greek law would not permit us to own property on Patmos. The island was frontier territory, just off the Turkish coast, and the Greek government was keen to prevent its real estate from passing into foreign (and possibly Turkish) hands. So only Greeks could own houses on Patmos. The well-heeled foreigners who had bought up large houses in Chora had, we were told, entered into complicated and expensive arrangements involving the formation of companies with Greek directors to whom the houses were registered. It was rather out of our league. A few wide-eyed outsiders had handed over their purchase money for the houses they wanted to buy to Greek "friends," but the consequences were not encouraging. In short, the situation was that prices were prohibitive; multiple ownership made purchasing a nightmare; and we were not allowed to own a house even if we found one. Felicia pressed eagerly ahead.

There was one official estate agent on the island. His name was Manios and he ran a small shop at the monastery selling guidebooks and postcards. As he had been born and brought up in America, he spoke the English he had learned there, which made life easier. Manios said he had no doubts he could fix us up with something, and told us of a few properties just on the market. For a week or so we turned up at appointments to view these houses, but somehow we never managed to cross a threshold. The owner of one was keen to sell but his cousins, who had a share in the property, would not be persuaded; another had just put the house on the market on an impulse and had a contrary impulse on the morning of our appointment and taken it off again; a third wanted to sell his house but refused to tell anybody that he wanted to sell it and canceled our appointment because the secret would be out. We were to discover why real estate dealings on Patmos tended to be furtive.

Finally we were told of a mansion. At least, we were told it was rather grand, and that it had been built by one of the wealthy shipowners who had lived in Chora in the eighteenth century. The owners were happy to sell and lived in Athens, so Manios took us to the property. Off a narrow cobbled street in the center of the town, a padlocked door led into an open space with a magnificent view over the port. Beyond it were the high dark hills of Samos and over to the right, through the summer haze, the twin peaks on the Turkish coast. It was a wide, sweeping view, unimpeded by buildings. I mentioned to Manios that this rather worried me, since we had come to buy one. He pointed out a low stone construction in a corner with walls a meter thick and heavy crossbeams that had once supported a ceiling. "The kitchen!" he announced.

The rest of the house, it seemed, had fallen victim to earthquakes and gales down through the centuries, and much of the stone had been taken away and used elsewhere in Chora. This was, Manios explained, good news for us because the site had been cleared without any expense to us for whatever reconstruction we cared to plan. The price for this picturesque ruin was exactly twice what we could afford, but Manios assured us it would be a good investment because pirates had frequently infested Patmos in the past and there was sure to be treasure buried in the garden. We were not enthused.

Sister Paraskevi enjoyed our tales of house hunting and decided to join us in the search. But she cannily pointed out that spring was not the season to buy. In the spring, all property owners are flushed with optimism at the prospect of the usual thousands of tourists who visit Patmos, fall in love with it and decide to spend the rest of their lives here. It often takes the whole summer for them to become aware of the problems and finally give up. As autumn settles in and the flood of would-be immigrants dwindles to a trickle, the daydreams of untold riches fade and people who want to sell their houses are more open to offers. We should come back in the autumn, she told us.

BACK IN ENGLAND, I spent a lot of the rest of the summer at the London Library, searching out books on Orthodoxy. After our experiences on Patmos, I had reached the position of accepting that Eastern Christianity could have remarkable and admirable effects on some people but that this did not, of course, guarantee its truth. I rejected the notion that there could be merit in believing something for which the evidence was rationally unconvincing. Then I came across the Russians.

The Western Christian apologists I had most admired— William Temple, Ronald Knox, Cardinal Newman—were all men of great intelligence with fluent and captivating writing styles who had been unshakably convinced of the truths they taught for the whole of their adult lives. I remember reading with some dismay, in the early pages of Newman's *Apologia*— surely one of the most moving and gracefully written of books— that Newman was convinced at the age of fifteen of the truth of Christian dogma with a certainty that had never been effaced or obscured. And that he was more sure of his election to eternal glory than that he had hands and feet. This gave the rest of the book an exotic appeal, such as the memoirs of a Watusi witch doctor might have had, but it made the argument, to an unbeliever, less relevant.

The Russian Orthodox apologists, on the other hand, had often experienced a change of heart in their adult lives. And nobody is more aware of the flaws in a philosophy than those who have embraced it, proclaimed it and then spotted its weaknesses. The Russian intellectuals who had gone through a rationalist phase and then turned to Christianity were intriguing to me because I had long accepted that increasing education and philosophical awareness led in the opposite direction.

Then again, in the early nineteenth century, when the ideals of the Enlightenment were being enthusiastically embraced in Western Europe, a Russian scholar had suddenly seen through them, and he wrote a searing critique.

Ivan Kireyevsky's father was a Freemason and an enthusiast for the Enlightenment, his mother a leading light in the literary salon circles of Moscow. They sent him to Berlin, where he studied with Hegel and Schelling before returning to Russia with a mission to free its citizens from the primitive credulity of the Orthodox Church. But he could find neither a publisher for his progressive ideas nor an academic job. He left Moscow and settled on his country estate, which happened to be close to Optina Pustin, a monastery famous for its spiritual fathers. Kireyevsky visited them, experienced a change of perspective and began to read the Greek Fathers. In their writings, he said, he found all that was most important and true in Schelling's philosophy developed more fully and stated more exactly. (This statement will be unsurprising to those familiar with Schelling's writings, since for most of his lifetime very few people—including the great German nature philosopher himself—were able to form a very clear idea of what he was trying to say.) Kireyevsky realized that the writings of the Greek Fathers were of abiding and not just historical interest.

Kireyevsky was received into the Orthodox Church and explained his reasoning in a critique of Western Christianity and Western philosophy which I found cogent and persuasive. The problems of Western Christianity, he wrote, had to do with authority. The Scholastic theologians such as St. Thomas Aquinas, under the influence of Aristotle, had erected a system of legalistic dogma that went far beyond Christian tradition. This meant that they could no longer claim the authority of tradition and had to locate authority in the hierarchy of the Catholic Church. The Protestant Reformation rejected that authority and replaced it with scripture. But scripture, being individually interpreted, had spawned a thousand different sects and eventually the rejection of faith. Russia had escaped the rationalism and legalism that the spirit of Ancient Rome, through the papacy, had imposed on the Western Church and so had no Reformation rebelling against it. The Orthodox Church, then, was the closest thing to the original.

Western philosophy had also been undermined by Aristotle, who identified human reason as the sole instrument in the search for truth. This had forced Western philosophers into an impotent rationalism that could locate truth only in the concatenations of logical argument and abstract thought. Kireyevsky proposed what he called "integral cognition," which put a person into contact with reality and with other people rather than any process of abstract thinking. This cognition combined reason and emotion, aesthetic sense and spiritual sensitivity into a general faculty that alone, he felt, should be accepted as the arbiter of truth.

I had long believed that the sole arbiter of truth was human reason, unclouded by emotion. The notion that reason should unite itself with irrational faculties and impulses seemed slightly dotty. But I had been impressed by the ideas of Hindu philosophers who insisted that intuition could throw light into dark places which reason was unable to penetrate. They did not reject reason; they simply said it had to occasionally be supplemented.

The book that most impressed me that summer is accepted as perhaps the most important work on Orthodox theology of the twentieth century: *The Mystical Theology of the Eastern Church,* by Vladimir Lossky. This is a complex work with a simple argument. Since the matters with which theology is ultimately concerned are beyond human understanding, all theology must be based on mysticism if it is to contain truth. And all mysticism must be theologically structured if it is to communicate. The theology of the Orthodox Church is apophatic; that is to say, it seeks to explain God not by making positive statements about Him but by negations. All positive statements about God must be untrue. If we say He is good, compassionate, merciful, etc., such statements must be inadequate when judged by human standards, the only ones we know. And even if we say that God exists, the statement is untrue if we mean that He is an existent object among many.

Again the Hindu philosophers came to mind, with their *"neti, neti"* ("not this, not that") attempt to describe the Brahman in the Upanishads. So often, Orthodox Christianity seemed to reflect more ancient religious ideas. I was finding it increasingly attractive as a creation of the moral imagination, like the Arthurian legends, the Norse gods or the Greek myths. But Orthodox Christianity seemed to me as remote from reality as they.

All this time I was looking forward to autumn, when I could return to Patmos to experience more of its effects and possibly even find a house that would tie us more closely to that extraordinary island.

Four

⌒ A Local Habitation

In late September we set off on a second visit to Patmos. Again we booked a package tour for a couple of weeks, during which time Felicia felt confident that with the help of whatever divine agencies might be disposed to take an interest in us we should find a house. The focus of these agencies was, of course, Sister Paraskevi. We headed straight for the Convent of Evangelismos on the morning after our arrival.

She greeted us with the news that a very suitable place was available: small, compact, with its own garden and, best of all, outside Chora, on the path down to Evangelismos and only a few hundred yards from the front gate of the convent. We could easily stroll down every morning for matins. The house was an old stone cottage "in need of sympathetic restoration" which belonged to a friend of hers. She took us there at once. It had neither piped water nor electricity, but Sister Paraskevi was sure they could be arranged. The house was solidly built and consisted of one room divided into three by stone partitions. A jagged crack running down the masonry at one end suggested subsidence, but since it had been there as long as anyone could remember, the ground seemed to have stabilized.

We were not put off by the crack, nor the three sunbathing adders which Felicia startled on the path to the house, nor even by the rumor that the adjoining plot had been sold to a "rich American"—a phrase deemed tautological on the island—who planned a hotel. But the price, alas, was almost as high as that of the ruined mansion, and far more than we could afford.

It was not in Sister Paraskevi's nature to be deflected from a task undertaken because it was impossible. She was convinced the Lord would provide, though for some time it was unclear whether He would do so by sending us money or a cheaper house. Three days before the end of our stay was the Feast of St. Thomas. This is a special day of celebration at the monastery because the skull of the apostle is kept there. I felt it a special day for me because doubting Thomas had always been the follower of Christ with whom I felt the greatest sympathy—he always asked for proof when proof was needed. So we went up to the ceremonies at the monastery, and when the holy relic was circulated among the crowd and presented to me, I followed the example of everybody else and kissed it. Until that moment I had, as I have said, always refused to perform any of the pious gestures that are second nature to the

Orthodox and the basest superstition to the Western rationalist. I still don't know whether my rationalism was weakening
or whether I was just scared to be seen as different. The skull
passed on.

The next day Sister Paraskevi had news. A devout Christian couple in Chora was hoping to move to Athens to buy a flat
there. They first had to sell their house, which was small but
habitable. The husband would be attending a liturgy at 6 A.M.
the following morning at a small chapel in a wood near the
Theological College. We should meet him there and the business would be settled with the help of Father Amphilochios,
who would be taking the liturgy.

The rendezvous appealed to my curiosity, as Father
Amphilochios was a legend on the island. He had been the spiritual child of the great Father Amphilochios Makris, founder of
the convent, and had taken his name. He taught theology at the
Theological College and, it was said, always secretly distributed
his salary to the poor. He lived an austere life and refused all possessions. The islanders told me they had a game which involved
giving him a small gift such as a ballpoint pen, which he would
always receive gratefully, and then lay bets on how long it took
him to pass it on to somebody else. As he had served as a missionary in the French colonies of West Africa, he spoke French. I was
keen to meet such a saintly character. We also had forty-eight
hours left on Patmos in which to buy a house.

We had a restless night. Could we rely in real estate matters on the judgment of a nun who spent her days in prayer
behind the walls of her convent? If the devout Christian couple
was really prepared to sell the house for half what Manios said

was the going price for a ruin, what was wrong with it? Did they in fact own it or would half a dozen cousins suddenly appear and make demands just when we thought we were secure? And where was the house? There were no glue factories in Chora, but it could be next to an abattoir or, worse, a disco.

We got up at half past five and walked down the donkey track to the chapel. The door was open into a tiny room, only three paces from the west door to the iconostasis. Candles were lit and the curtains were closed across the royal doors. Only two boys were standing inside, probably theological students, who were softly chanting, alternately, the Jesus prayer: "*Kirie, Jesus Christe, eleison me, ton amartalon*" ("Lord Jesus Christ, have mercy on me, a sinner"). We stood just inside the door and waited. After a while the curtains were drawn back and a priest appeared in the sanctuary. Father Amphilochios.

The liturgy was scrupulously performed. I remember thinking it strange that the priest should read from a service book throughout when he must have performed the ritual thousands of times and be word-perfect in it. But the Orthodox Church is so careful to preserve its traditions without alteration that the practice is always for a priest to read the words from a service book. Perhaps this also emphasizes that the words are not his own. Catholic friends have told me that, as children, they used to set a stopwatch on the priests and go for the one who could get through the mass in the shortest time. They would point out that the priest's final words are "*Ite, missa est*" ("Go. It is finished") and that the congregation members then reply with relief, "*Deo gratias*" ("Thank God!"). The Orthodox seem more measured about their worship, though I noticed that people seemed free to wander in and out during the liturgy and that it was only during moments of high drama that everyone's attention was exclusively focused on what was going on.

After the liturgy we went out into the brightness of a clear autumn morning. The chapel was surrounded by trees and in the shade of one, on a rocky outcrop, sat the fattest man I had ever seen. Not the largest—he was only about five feet four inches tall—but his waistline seemed (and, I later discovered, actually was) the same measurement. He was clean-shaven, with close-cropped gray hair and a ready grin. His name was Stelios, and he wanted to sell his house.

Father Amphilochios came out of the church and sat with us on the rocks. There are few variables in describing the appearance of Greek priests, perhaps only height, girth and color of beard. He was middling in all these, the beard being black, flecked with gray. But his eyes were amazingly expressive, firstly because of their concentration—you knew when he looked at you that he was seeing only you—and then because of their power to convey emotion: curiosity, compassion, anger, delight. He said that Sister Paraskevi had told him about us: that Felicia was Orthodox but I was not and that we wanted to buy a house on Patmos. Stelios, he told us, was an old friend and parishioner, and a good man. He had worked for the British for many years as an engineer in Egypt and spoke a sort of English. He wanted to leave Patmos and settle near Athens to live out his retirement near the bright lights. Would we like to buy his house?

Felicia, who has a certain impatience with circumvention, leapt into the conversation at this point, saying, "Yes we would, but we have only six million drachmas," thus revealing our hand. "Six million!" said Stelios. "For that you can have the house and everything that's in it!" And he held out his hand.

Father Amphilochios spread his palms in a gesture I took to mean that the matter had been providentially supervised. I shook Stelios's extended hand because it would have been offensive to leave it hanging there unacknowledged. Felicia's eyes shone with excitement, Father Amphilochios nodded benignly, Stelios grinned and I was filled with black panic. We had solemnly agreed, sitting on a rock in the middle of a wood, to give all the money we possessed to a man we had just met in return for some unspecified rights, which fell short of ownership, to a house we had not seen. True, Father Amphilochios was clearly a man of honor, and he seemed well pleased. It would have been churlish, if not impudent or even blasphemous, to have doubts. But I managed to ask diffidently if, perhaps, we could, at some convenient time, take a look at the house we had just bought.

Stelios immediately invited us all there for coffee and, Father Amphilochios having other business, Felicia and I walked with him along the short track through the woods to the road which climbs from Scala to Chora. There we sat on a low wall and Stelios said that he would arrange for a car to take us up the mountain. The arrangement was not complicated. We simply sat there for a couple of minutes and the next car that approached stopped to pick us up. Everybody on Patmos knew Stelios. They called him *"O Chondros"*—"the Fat Man"—and accepted that he could not walk more than a few hundred yards. So if he needed a lift he would simply sit by a roadside until somebody picked him up. And somebody always did.

We got out of the car at the bus station in Chora, where the road ends, and began the slow walk through the narrow cobbled streets. Stelios chatted exuberantly as we walked. I was unresponsive, sick with apprehension as we approached each tumbledown ruin, expecting Stelios to force open the remnants of a door and invite us in to a heap of rubble and a Primus stove on a tea chest, which would constitute the kitchen. We turned, to our surprise, at the corner of Marouso's house and went down a narrow lane we knew well. At the bottom was a high whitewashed stone wall and set in the wall was a green metal door. Stelios hammered on this and shouted a stream of what sounded like abuse. A neat, nervous woman with gray hair swept back from her face and tied tightly in a bun cautiously opened the door. She was wearing a checkered apron over the black dress that all respectable ladies above the age of forty seem to favor on Patmos.

Stelios introduced Katerina, his wife, and told her we had bought their house. She seemed pleased. It was important that she should be, because the house turned out to be hers. The custom on Patmos is that houses usually belong to the women of the island, a sensible way of giving them security, since for centuries their men have gone off to sea or to work in foreign lands, without always returning. Katerina spoke no English but gestured that we should come in and look around. We only later realized how much this gesture cost her. She was very house-

proud and would have liked a week's notice to scrub the place
down before our arrival.

It needed no preening. The house and garden were immaculate. We went down a few stone steps into a courtyard
paved with old red Patmian tiles and shaded by an olive tree.
Off the courtyard to one side was a kitchen with a stainless-steel
sink, a gas cooker set in an old oven alcove and a venerable refrigerator with a curved door six inches thick. Off the kitchen
was a bathroom containing a shower and lavatory and on the
wall a white cupboard with a red cross painted on the door: the
family medicine cabinet. The door was slightly open and I peered
nosily inside to check on local first-aid precautions. The cupboard contained only two items: a set of worry beads and an icon
of the Mother of God.

Across the courtyard, fly-screened doors opened into a
narrow room, only six feet across, with two chairs and a small
table in the corner. On the table was a television set, and I was
delighted to see that attached to the aerial was a blue glass bead
I recognized as the charm that wards off the evil eye. It couldn't
have been better sited. I asked Stelios if he would please take
the television to Athens.

In the wall that separated this narrow room from a large
dark room beyond was a low door and, surprisingly to us, a window. But to have a window opening in an internal wall is in fact
common on the island; it helps the circulation of breeze during
the hot summers. We went into the larger room and found a
wardrobe, a double bed and a dining table. In the courtyard,
stone steps led to a south-facing veranda, just large enough for
a table and two chairs and leading to a bedroom, in the corner

of which were double doors with glass panels. These doors led to a narrow room like the one downstairs, but instead of the television there was a small iconostasis in the corner, with oil lamps burning on it. From one of the beams a plank of wood swung suspended by ropes, and on the plank were several dishes of cheese.

By now all my anxieties had drained away and I felt as elated as Felicia looked. The house was beautifully kept, the walls were thick, the roofs showed no sign of leakage. We went back down into the courtyard to discover a wellhead with a small bucket and a neatly coiled rope standing by it. Stelios lifted off the wooden cover and shone a torch down to reveal a stone-lined chamber twenty feet deep, as wide as the courtyard above it and filled with perfectly clear water. He then took us through a doorway in the southern wall of the courtyard into a garden with an olive and a fig tree, and leading the way through to a second garden, proudly gestured toward his bid for self-sufficiency: row upon row of flourishing onions. The property stood above an open valley, across which stood the mountain and hermitage of Prophet Elias.

Over coffee, Stelios explained that we must say nothing about our plans to buy the house. He reassured us that the property belonged to Katerina exclusively so there would be no problems in executing the sale, but said that if any of her relatives were to hear about it they would immediately beat a path to her door to share in the proceeds. It would be difficult to deny them, and Stelios and Katerina needed the money to buy their flat in Athens, so we must keep the secret until they were safely on the ferry. They would be ready to leave on May 1 of the following year, and we could take over the house on that date.

One other point: since they had no truck with banks, we should pack the six million in cash into a plastic bag and, ideally, hand it to them as they walked up the ferry gangway. Stelios's notions of real estate transactions seemed to have a breezy informality quite different from the way these matters are ordered in England; but we were on Patmos, planned to spend a lot of our time there and had to get used to Patmian ways. At least we had found a wonderful house, agreed upon the price and date of closing with the owners and still had one day of our holiday left during which to relish the prospect.

But the one consistency in Patmian affairs we had yet to learn is that nothing can be counted on.

The next day we decided to take the donkey path from Chora to Scala. Sooner or later—usually sooner—all visitors to Patmos hear about this challenge, usually from one of the Old Hands, who constitute one of the social hazards of Patmos and are an ever-present threat to the new arrival. They have been coming to the island every year for decades and insist on turning every conversation around to the point where they can utter the dread words: "When I first came to Patmos . . ." These words should be one's signal to remember something urgent that has to be done elsewhere. They are the introit to a litany of complaints about the current decadence, ecological devastation, architectural perversity and dietary waywardness of the island. The Old Hands long for the days when the peasantry was picturesquely poor and knew its place, when they were welcomed in every Greek household with a crust of wholesome bread, a slice of feta cheese from the goats that peacefully grazed the garden and a glass of homemade wine trodden out by humble feet ennobled by honest toil. One of the regular clichés of these latter-day Tolstoys is "When I first came to Patmos, we had to climb to the monastery up the donkey track—on donkeys!"

The donkeys have gone but the donkey track is still there and a pleasure to walk, though the journey is a lot easier down-hill. It begins in the main square of Chora, which is bounded by the town hall. The hall still has a painted sign on the front of the building in large black capitals proclaiming it to be a rural doctor's surgery, though it is many years since a medical practice operated there. The main square is commonly called Xanthos Square because there is a larger-than-life bronze bust on a stone plinth of Emmanuel Xanthos, born on Patmos and one of the three cofounders of the Friendly Society, which rallied opposition to the Turks and launched the rebellion of 1821. In fact, the real Xanthos Square, which has a small plaque on the side of a tiny house to prove it, is located down a short cobbled street to the west of the statue; but the larger space has the memorial and has taken over the name.

The donkey track is made up of rocks the size of footballs set into the earth, forming a cobbled road about twelve to fifteen feet across. It heads due north toward Scala and is crossed at intervals by a zigzagging asphalt road. When it intersects the road, the donkey track does not always start up again immediately opposite itself and is easy to lose, but a careful glance to the right or left will pick it up again. One of the minor pleasures of walking down the track is to be constantly reminded, by the purple faces of the people you meet struggling in the opposite direction, how right you were not to be walking up it. Only the robust should attempt the climb.

A major attraction of the walk down is that you are facing a superb view all the way. As well as the wide sweep of islands to the north, there is the harbor of Scala, with its ferries and tourist ships tied up alongside the quay or anchored out; busy *kaiki* launches ferrying passengers; tiny, gaily painted fishing boats bobbing out to the fishing grounds around the island; and often a yacht or two nosing into the harbor, the more skilled still under sail.

About halfway down the track you pass the Patmian School, its twin flags proclaiming with blue and white stripes loyalty to Greece and with the yellow twin-headed eagle allegiance to Constantinople. The original school was founded in 1713 by a scholarly deacon of the monastery, Makarios Kaloyeras, and built up such a reputation that, in 1731, a Russian visitor described it as having, for the Greeks under Turkish yoke, "the significance of ancient Athens." It produced distinguished academics, bishops, even patriarchs, as well as political leaders, including Emmanuel Xanthos. The original school was close to the Monastery of the Apocalypse, but the Italians closed it down and the new buildings, which were funded by Patmians in the U.S. as well as by the monastery, were built fifty meters up the hill in 1947. It is still a center of theological instruction for the whole of Greece. If its students, who are often seen wandering up and down the donkey path, do not seem overburdened with piety, it should be remembered that in Greece theological studies are not just for would-be priests: theology, being an important aspect of human learning, is part of a general education.

Below the school the donkey track is shaded for a hundred yards or so by tall eucalyptus trees, then meets the asphalt road at a junction dominated by a white-domed church high in a compound to the left. There are low flat-roofed modern buildings in the compound and a small rusting blue sign in its fence with no words but just a crude painting of a black iron bed with a red cross over it. This is the hospital. The dominance of the church here always reminds me of the contents of Katerina's medicine cabinet: prayer beads and an icon.

Shortly after the hospital the path enters the outer suburbs of Scala, where the modern concrete block houses begin. But nestled between these tall faceless constructions are tiny old stone cottages, their gardens a chaos of colors, with heaps of red geraniums spilling out into the street, purple bougainvillea swamping the walls, pink and white roses pushing their heads through a riot of honeysuckle. The dead hand of modern suburbia is kept at bay by these survivors and by the fields— not gardens, but fields—of tomatoes, aubergines, peppers and potatoes that are holding their own in the expanding wasteland of concrete.

By now the donkey track has itself been submerged under asphalt and become one of the streets of the town. On the very last sharp bend, there is a tiny church standing on the right below the level of the street which is obviously a place of importance. Nobody passes it without making the sign of the cross, even if they are mothers on motorbikes with two children and a heap of shopping. This church has the reputation of being the oldest in Scala. It is dedicated to the Holy Spirit and to an Egyptian father, Paisios the Great, who was famous for his wisdom and a rather dispiriting capacity to go without food. His biographer, St. John the Dwarf, records that he regularly went without eating for periods of seventy days. There is a distinctly gaunt icon of the saint on the iconostasis of this little church, which seems to admonish the traveler entering the fleshpots of the port.

Not that Scala is given to riotous living. There is, indeed, a rather severe notice on the wall of the customhouse to catch the eye of tourists arriving by sea: "WE ARE A HOLY ISLAND. RESPECT OUR TRADITIONS." And, indeed, Patmos was declared to be a Holy Island by Act of Parliament, though by what authority a secular body of politicians could declare a place to be consecrated, sacred, belonging to or empowered by God is not clear. The issue was brought into rather sharp focus in 1988 when a local businessman paid for the erection of a bronze statue to Poseidon, god of the sea, on the quay. Rather less than life-sized, he was in the traditional pose: naked and about to throw a trident. The island was immediately divided between those who thought it absolutely right that the first figure to catch the eye of visitors arriving by sea to a Greek island should be the Greek god who had supervised their journey and those who held that Patmos was more than just a Greek island, but a Christian island where the Greek gods were no longer in charge. After a week of wrangling, the statue quietly disappeared one night. The Christians had won.

But the Christians do not have things entirely their own way in Scala. Some of the slogans on T-shirts and picture postcards for sale in the tourist shops do little to promote piety and there

is nothing in the atmosphere of a busy port to suggest that it is
the entrance to a place of pilgrimage. Occasional processions
of middle-aged people in dark suits and sensible dresses wend
their way through the streets with a priest in attendance, but
the summer population of Scala is basically the same as that
of any Greek seaside town: barefoot backpackers, tanned nut-
brown and strung about with beads; package-tour victims
from the cold cities of the north with chalk-white legs and
angry red shoulders; earnest groups with team leaders and
guidebooks contrasting with the jollier crowd who throng the
bars and think of abroad as where you go to anesthetize the
frontal lobes.

    Scala provides for all of these. In fact, Scala is the provider
of Patmos: it has the post office, the police station, the bank,
the customhouse, the travel agents and most of the hotels. If
Chora was built by rich shipowners with an educated sense of
how to spend money, Scala was built by businessmen whose
priority was to make it. So most of the buildings are functional:
the quayside cafés converted from warehouses, and the modern shops set in rows that face each other across a narrow street.
It seems odd to me that the shops which sell tat to the tourists
should announce themselves as "tourist shops," since most tourists would prefer to buy things from what they would see as the
genuine local stores. But they thrive, I suppose, because so many
visitors to Patmos have money to spend and only a limited time
in which to spend it. So it helps to have the bits and pieces with
the name "Patmos" on them under a single roof or several adjoining ones.

But Scala is not Patmos. It is the island's first point of contact with international tourism, a frontier town under regular assault by the forces of barbarism from across the sea. It provides the bread and circuses; there is a lot of fun to be had there. But as Scala reminds us that there is a world too busy to be aware of realities that might exist outside itself, Patmos hints at those realities and even manages to suggest that they may be the ultimate ones.

Five

☞ Testing Times

At the end of April 1988, we set off for Greece on yet another two-week package tour. We intended to stay for at least six months to take over and do up the house, but such were the insanities of air ticketing that a package return ticket was half the price of a regular single fare. So the travel agent told us to buy the return ticket and throw away the return half.

We went straight to our old room at Marouso's house on arrival, expecting to be there for a couple of days or so until Stelios and Katerina left, as arranged, on May 1, when we could move over and start our new life. Having dropped our bags at Marouso's, we walked straight down to Stelios's house to make sure all was going well and to offer a hand with the packing.

Though Stelios greeted us heartily enough, Katerina looked nervous and depressed. I thought at first that this was brought on by the prospect of leaving everything that was familiar and heading for a more abrasive life in Athens; but it was soon obvious that something was wrong.

Stelios sat us down and, while Katerina prepared the coffee, chatted about the weather they'd had the past winter and how grateful he was for the warm trousers (waist 64", length 25") we had sent from England. He waited until the coffee arrived before blowing away our dreams. Katerina, he explained, had always had problems with her breathing. When he had visited Athens a few weeks before to look for a flat in the suburbs, he had had his first experience of the pollution there. You could taste the sulfur at the back of your throat—appropriate gagging noises—and he thought he was going to be very ill. He knew that many Athenians were carted off to hospital with breathing difficulties every summer and that some of them died. His conscience would not let him put Katerina at risk. They had decided they should stay on Patmos.

I could see that Felicia was sick with disappointment. But she put a hand on Katerina's and said we understood. Of course, we were sad to have lost the chance of living in their very special house, but we did not want to be responsible for her falling ill in Athens. We would keep up our search for a home on Patmos and hope that we could continue to be friends and, perhaps, even neighbors. As Felicia spoke, I could see that Katerina did not seem at all comforted—in fact, she was getting even more agitated. And Stelios, instead of looking relieved that we were letting him out of a solemn agreement sealed by a handshake in the presence of a priest, dropped his eyes, furrowed his brow and looked as though our attempts to be friendly were only making the situation worse.

Clearly we were not reacting as they'd expected. I was frantically trying to remember whether or not we had thrown away the return half of our air tickets as we stood up to leave. But when we reached the door Katerina let out a little cry and rushed into the kitchen. Stelios shouted that we should sit down again for another cup of coffee and joined her. It was obvious from the sounds emerging that they were having a difference of opinion and that it was over something important. Moreover, it had something to do with us. We had said something that had upset both of them and could not work out what it might be. Neither of us wanted more coffee. All we could think of was getting back to our room and searching the bags for those return air tickets.

When they came out, Stelios explained that they had talked over the matter of Katerina's health and decided that they really shouldn't disappoint us and that she was, perhaps, more robust than he had thought. They would, after all, go ahead with the deal—and he had, in fact, arranged to buy a flat in Athens. Unfortunately, they could not occupy it until June 1. Even more unfortunately, they had to pay for it straightaway. So could we please give them the money immediately and wait for another month to take over the house? And, by the way, did I not think that "six and a half million" had a finer ring to it than just "six"?

The scales fell away. Of course, Stelios had dreamed up the idea that Katerina was too sick to go to Athens because he thought we would respond like normal human beings by screaming for our rights; then we should have been open to renegotiations.

Katerina was depressed and nervous not over the prospect of going to Athens, but over the possibility of missing the chance to get away. The flat had been bought, the arrangements made; Stelios simply wanted to improve on his price. I told him truthfully that six was all we had, and we finished our coffees amicably enough.

There remained the question of how we could, with any hope of something approaching security, arrange to hand over the money before moving into the house. This was a matter for the notary public, and we decided that we should begin the daunting process of complex legal negotiations, in Greek, as soon as we felt strong enough. It would be prudent to do so before the date of our return air tickets in case it didn't work out. But first we had to find a Greek in whose name the property could be registered. As foreigners, we could have no legal title. The law allowed us simply to pay for the house, which would be registered to somebody local on the understanding that if the law ever changed, that somebody, without any legal obligation to do so, would hand it back. It was not an arrangement for the fainthearted.

We asked Father Amphilochios if he could suggest somebody on the island and could not believe our luck when he volunteered himself. By another happy accident, we met a friend who told us the notary public was leaving early the following morning for a holiday in America, so we rushed to her office and arranged a panic appointment for that evening. We met Father Amphilochios at the Theological College after work and walked together down the donkey track to Scala. Stelios and Katerina had arranged to take the bus so that nobody would see us together and guess what was going on. Our progress was slow because everyone Father Amphilochios met insisted on demonstrating at length his or her joy at the meeting, and he was too sensitive to ever give the impression to anyone that he might have more important things to do elsewhere.

Even the notary public, an intimidating official, seemed to thaw with pleasure when we entered her office, and sent out her secretary for coffee and sweets. It took the usual ten minutes or so for her to exchange with Father Amphilochios information as to the health, current marital status, numbers of offspring, drinking habits and prospects of their extended families, and then we got down to business. She immediately threw up her arms with frustration and despair at the stupidity of the lay public and pointed out that Father Amphilochios, being a monk, could not own property without breaking his vow of poverty. Even if a way could be found around this obstacle—and she hinted that it was not unprecedented—we should realize that if the good father were to be untimely called to his Maker, the house would revert immediately and irrevocably to the monastery.

The loss of Father Amphilochios as someone to whom we could safely hand over our house was serious. We had not been long enough on the island to know whom we could trust and it was obvious that our other close friend, Sister Paraskevi, would, as a nun, be disqualified from stepping into the breach. Fortunately the decision was not left to us. Father Amphilochios heard what the notary public said, smiled, stepped through the open door into the street, stopped a passerby and brought her into the office. "Argiri Roussaki," he introduced, "an old friend of mine. You can write the house to her."

Saintly persons make the rest of us uneasy at times. They have, I had discovered on Patmos, this habit of finding sermons in stones and good in everything. Father Amphilochios, I thought meanly, would have found it in his heart to give a character reference to Vlad the Impaler. I forgot to mention that, before setting off for Scala that evening, we had offered him money for the upkeep of his little chapel in the woods as a token of gratitude for his help. He told us to leave it on a plate inside the door of the chapel. We pointed out that the door was always open and that any passerby could easily take the money. "If anybody takes the money," he said simply, "it must be because they need it."

This sort of shining benevolence does not inspire confidence in a secularized character from the materialistic West who is being asked to hand over all his money to a complete stranger with no security at all. Argiri Roussaki, for all I knew, could have been running drugs. And even if she were a model housewife, would her virtue stand the test of a free house and the temptation to forget to hand it back if and when the time came for us to ask her?

She exuded piety: short, middle-aged, dressed entirely in black, with a severe face that lit up from time to time with a shining smile. We liked her immediately, and there was in any case no alternative: Father Amphilochios had made the decision and we had to go along with it. Besides, the notary public was leaving the island the next morning, so there would be no second chance. "Our" house was registered in the name of Argiri Roussaki and we stood by as the papers were signed agreeing to transfer the legal ownership to her when we handed over the money to Katerina.

Still sworn to secrecy, we were waiting outside the door of the bank when it opened the next day. The manager didn't blink when we showed him our draft on an English bank and asked for six million drachmas, in notes, to be packed into a plastic shopping bag. He even spent some time on the phone trying, he said, to find the most favorable rate of exchange and astonished us with the news that the drachma had nosedived during the night and we had a tidy little bonus on top. This affluence was to be short-lived.

We handed over the shopping bag to Stelios on a street corner and went our separate ways. Part of the compact of secrecy he insisted on was that we should not be seen together too much in case people began to suspect. Now we could only sit back and wait.

May 1988 was the longest month of the century. We spent it drawing plans of each room in our house and organizing on paper the disposition of furniture. We even worked out how to spend our bonus from the exchange on extra items—until we heard about the tax. Nobody had mentioned that if you buy a house, you pay tax. Nor that both the vendor and the purchaser have to pay. Nor that the Greek custom is that if the vendor is Greek and the purchaser from abroad, the purchaser pays both taxes.

We were told about this during the longest month. Our informant tried to reassure us by pointing out that the tax is based on the amount paid for the house. And that nobody in his right mind ever admits the real figure. The tax man knows this and makes his own assessment of the value, helped by photographs of the property. So we had to arrange for a set of photographs to be taken at noon, the least photogenic time, from unflattering angles and preferably slightly out of focus. We followed this advice, using a cheap camera and an unskilled operator, but because a priest had arranged our house purchase, we did not have the liberty to lie about the price. The tax man, assuming we had, upped the figure of six million to seven and a half. But our exchange bonus managed to cope.

May crawled by, and we spent the days swimming with our daughter and her boyfriend, who had arranged to come out to help us move into the house. The delay meant that instead of the joys of humping furniture they had to be content with lazing about on beaches. Every day we looked across at our little house from the veranda at Marouso's, and one early morning near the end of the month we saw a large lorry parked on the road that ran through the valley below the house and watched the driver and Stelios carrying pieces of furniture down the narrow path and loading them. We had thought that these were ours but couldn't object, as we were not supposed to have any contact with him. But we didn't really mind. We were so delighted at the prospect of moving in we didn't much care what we found there.

Stelios left for Athens on the truck with the furniture, but Katerina stayed in the house. All was silent there for a couple of days, until the first of June finally arrived and we mustered the courage to knock on the door to claim our property. Katerina opened it—prim, neat, not a hair out of place. She invited us in and asked if we would like coffee. We accepted, although we both felt that as the place was now ours, it would have been more appropriate if we had invited her. She then took us round every room, and we suddenly understood why she had stayed behind when Stelios went off with the furniture. The house was immaculate: floors and windows polished, cushions fluffed up, fridge gleaming, even the cutlery and glasses scintillating. There were fresh roses from the garden in the bedroom and dozens of tiny knickknacks—souvenirs of Patmos in the form of ashtrays and statuettes—carefully dusted and placed on windowsills and tables. We remembered moving into places in England where it took a couple of days to clear out the rubbish left by the previous occupants, and were touched and grateful.

There were, of course, challenges ahead. To start with: electricity. Now, this is something the people of Patmos are proud of. It is generated on the island in a large warehouse near the harbor that vibrates day and night to the throb of huge engines. So proud is the electricity company of its product that the buildings of both Scala and Chora are festooned with the celebratory coils and loops of heavy black cable that announce its presence. No effort is spared to display these symbols of modernity, and our little house in Chora was lavishly embellished with them. But we soon noticed that every time the refrigerator started up the lights dimmed. This was disconcerting during the evening hours when you were trying to read. Adonis, the local electrician, told us that this was because the supply to our house was intended only for lights and not for power. So we asked him to change it. He did, even installing a water heater so that we could have hot showers.

But the first time I tried out the hot shower was almost my last. I'd stripped off and reached over the shower basin to turn on the metal tap when a spark leapt from the tap and shot up my arm to the shoulder. I know little about electricity, but I realized immediately that things were not as they should be in and around our shower. One thing I did remember was that though electricity likes water and would be concentrated if I took a shower in its presence, it doesn't like rubber, so I would be fine if I took the shower in rubber boots. We didn't have any actual Wellingtons with us, so I slipped on a pair of beach sandals with rubber soles and showered in them. It was a colorful experience, for although the tap gave only a rather pleasurable tingle when turned on, the water itself seemed to contain electricity, because blue flashes flickered across the insides of my eyelids when I blinked. Felicia tried out the shower in rubber sandals and reported the same experience.

Friends told us that we should not be taking daily showers, even in rubber shoes, if the taps were live. So I asked Adonis to fix the problem. That was when we first came up against a traditional Patmian device that was to become familiar. Adonis said the electricity supply was not properly earthed, so I should see the electricity company. When I went down to their offices in Scala and managed to speak to an engineer, he smiled sympathetically and said that since the problem was inside the house—that is, beyond the point at which the company's wiring stopped and the domestic wiring started—it was our responsibility. Why did I not ask my electrician to fix it? So back to Adonis, who was difficult to track down since he was the only electrician in Chora at the time and spent his days dashing between clamoring and disconnected housewives.

When I told him what the electricity company's man had said, he shook his head, looked at me as if I were the most unbelievably credulous simpleton, muttered the equivalent of "He would say that, wouldn't he" and promised to call round the following day. This was my first contact with what I came to realize was the unique vocabulary relating to time used by Patmian builders and technicians. The word *avrio,* which Adonis had used, does indeed mean "tomorrow" if you look it up in a dictionary. But here on Patmos, and if used in the context I have described, it is better translated as "about the middle of next week." The words *tin ali evdomatha,* which the dictionary will tell you mean "next week," here indicate "toward the end of next month." And the most dread words of all, *se liges meres,* which linguists tell you mean "in a few days," should properly be translated, when spoken by a Patmian builder or technician whose help is being sought: "I really haven't the faintest idea when."

So Adonis arrived about the middle of the following week and spent some time trying to convince me that our situation was no different from that of all people who take showers in Chora. The township is built, he explained, on rock. That means the copper earthing tubes used by the electricity company cannot be sunk to the required depth without an expensive drill. The electricity company is not fond of expenditure, so it merely taps the earthing tube along the surface. Ergo, the taps in the showers tingle and blue flashes entertain the closed eyes of bathers. I am very easily persuaded by technicians, partly because I hate confrontation and also because I have an overdeveloped faculty of rationalization. So I was ready to accept what Adonis said and even to attempt to persuade Felicia that mild doses of electric shock were used in therapy for rheumatic joints (although I also thought it might be nettle stings). But she would have none of it and pressed for a solution rather than an excuse.

Adonis managed to acquit himself of responsibility by connecting our supply to that of the neighbor, who had a garden and so was properly earthed. The taps ceased to tingle. I had proof that the electricity company was responsible and tackled them again, this time with Adonis alongside. They brought a drill and fixed the problem; I think it was *tin ali evdomatha* when they came. I quite missed the blue flashes.

SHOPPING ON A SMALL ISLAND is different. In England we make a list of what we need and do the rounds of the shops until all the items are ticked off. On Patmos this can be very time-consuming and frustrating because half the things are not here: "Tomatoes? Try on Thursday"; "Clear varnish? Saturday morning"; "Broad beans? Next February." Some of the vegetables, like the broad beans, have a short season and don't reappear until the following year. Cauliflower and cabbages are spasmodic and appear without notice, usually showing the signs of a long sea voyage. When real delicacies arrive, like strawberries and the first cherries of the season, the word spreads quickly and boxes are soon emptied. All in all, it seems best to forget menu planning and to simply see what is on offer, which has the stimulus of uncertainty and discovery but quite often results in monotony.

If you ask a shopkeeper for something and he smiles and raises both eyebrows, you probably think he is about to have the pleasure of serving you. In fact, the raised eyebrows mean no. The smile still has me puzzled. I used to think it was a malicious expression of the delight felt by people in authority who get the chance to frustrate you. But it is not unfriendly. In fact, the smile of negativity on Patmos is human, warm, compassionate. It seems to say: "I too go through life searching for things I cannot find. So many things that seem important to me are beyond my reach. I know your heart was set on the Coleman's mustard/five-volt fuse wire/biological washing powder, which I do not have right now. But we must smile, mustn't we? For life goes on . . ."

When we first settled in Chora we shopped with Lukas for vegetables and with Nikos, the supermarket, for everything else. Lukas was miscast as a greengrocer. He was shaped by nature to run a swanky casino in Casablanca. Small neat figure; gray hair slicked back from a sharp face with trim mustache; pants pressed to a knife edge; two-tone shoes; and always an elegant lit cigarette held between the ends of his first two delicate fingers. Lukas was an inconsistent greengrocer, since the part did not suit him. Sometimes he would vanish for days—the old wooden door under the archway would stay locked and the rumor would spread that Lukas was on another island, playing another role.

The idea of the supermarket was, like so many institutions of the Western world, originally Greek. The word for "grocery" here was—and it can still be found painted over the older stores—*pantopoleion,* which means, literally, "sells everything." The West did not adopt the supermarket until 1933, by which time the Greeks had been selling everything for generations. The scale is a little different, of course, but the range is wide, and we found that Nikos could supply most of our needs. We traveled to Scala only for meat and fish.

We usually walked down the donkey track to Scala and came back with the shopping by bus. The Patmos bus is one of the island's most remarkable traditions. There is only one; it travels once each day from one end of the island to the other (twice in summer) and makes regular trips from Scala to Chora and back from seven-thirty in the morning (and until as late as eleven at night during the summer). It is most remarkable for its punctuality, since few things start on time here, and its reliability. Throughout the summer months, even when the island population increases from two to twelve thousand and the boarding of the bus is like a scene from the Tokyo underground, it keeps going seven days a week. When it fills up for one leg of its journey around the island it will double back and repeat the trip and still manage to keep on time.

We used the bus regularly until one day we heard that the cargo ships from Japan to the Aegean islands were traveling out here with hundreds of clapped-out motor scooters as ballast. They had been taken off the roads of Japan because they were worn out, but were being bought up by an enterprising mechanic on Kalymnos who somehow mechanically rejuvenated them, then sold them off cheap to undemanding customers. We bought one. It ran smoothly for ten years.

Six

☞ To Kiss an Icon

Amphilochios, one of the saints of the Orthodox Church, operated as a successful lawyer in Constantinople during the early part of the fourth century. As a student, he was a friend of Basil, who was to become St. Basil the Great. Amphilochios tired early of the litigious life and its material rewards in the capital and settled in a remote cave, where he lived alone for forty years. When the city of Iconium, in Phrygia, where St. Paul had introduced Christianity on his first missionary journey, found itself without a bishop, Amphilochios was translated to the Episcopal throne. He spent the rest of his life defending the purity of the Orthodox faith.

There is a story that Emperor Theodosius the Great, who had a capricious relationship with his Christian subjects, called

Amphilochios one day into the imperial presence. The emperor
was sitting on the imperial throne, with his son, Arcadius, whom
he had made co-emperor at his side. Amphilochios did rever-
ence to Theodosius but completely ignored his son. The emperor
was furious and ordered Amphilochios to be driven from the
court. As the guards seized him, the saint stood his ground and
said: "Do you see, O Emperor, how you do not tolerate a slight
paid to your son? In the same way, God the Father does not
tolerate dishonor paid to His son, Jesus Christ, turning with
loathing from those who blaspheme against him . . ." The point
seems to have been taken, because Amphilochios survived the
emperor's displeasure, to die at a great age in 395.

The same intransigence in the face of authority was, as
we have seen, part of the character of Amphilochios Makris,
founder of the Convent of Evangelismos. His spiritual son,
Amphilochios Tsoukos, who had orchestrated our purchase
of a house in Chora, seemed all gentleness and love. His eyes
shone with enthusiasm for living, he laughed a lot, he touched
people close to him and whenever he was in public a crowd
surrounded him. Father Amphilochios was known on Patmos
as a man of great charity and compassion. But he had an in-
flexible core.

Soon after we met, I had the chance to talk to him about
Orthodox Christianity. The conversation was to alter my perspective on life, and I remember the setting clearly. We were
sitting again on the rocks outside his little chapel with the early
morning sun filtering through the trees. Felicia was there, patiently watching me falling into the mode she had seen so often,
that of *Everyman reporter*. I had spent the previous twelve

years interviewing religious leaders, and I recognized Father Amphilochios as a promising interviewee: he was firmly rooted in a primitive Christian faith which shaped his every waking hour; he seemed to combine a medieval austerity in his life with a renaissance enthusiasm for living. He was clearly a man whose priorities lay outside his immediate circumstances. Since he had experience as a missionary, spreading the Christian message among the tribal people of West Africa, it seemed fair to ask him about his techniques for enlightening unbelievers. I was one of them, and I was tackling him on behalf of liberal humanism.

I explained to him that I was a member of an enormous modern tribe that rejected the Christian message. This was not because we knew too little but because we knew too much. We understood the human psyche; we had analyzed the workings of the human mind, conscious and unconscious; we knew that religious faith was simply a compensatory mechanism that gave emotional reassurance to the insecure. We could not be deceived by myths, no matter how powerful their archetypal resonances. We sought the truth and, unlike Christians, saw no virtue in putting our trust in so-called realities for which there was insufficient evidence.

For the past three hundred years leading intellectuals of our tribe had examined the philosophical proofs for the existence of God and found them wanting. Our scholars had looked at the linguistic and archaeological evidence for biblical truths and had pronounced them flawed. Our biologists accepted a version of the story of life on earth that needed no external directing hand. So, we had abandoned Christianity after long and careful consideration of its claims and with some regret. That rejection was a consequence of our fearless pursuit of truth. "If you came," I said, "as a missionary to my tribe today, what would you say to us?" I sat back, conscious of having put him on the spot. He looked at me with a smile and said simply: "I would not say anything to you. I would simply live with you. And I would love you."

This was not the answer I expected from a theologian. I was looking forward to a friendly tussle over the five proofs for the existence of God or the claims of the early councils of the Church that Christ was truly man or truly divine. This was all familiar ground that I had worked over many times, and I was confident of holding my own as an unbeliever. When I heard those words from that man at that time, I experienced a shift in understanding. It was like the impact of great music. We all hear important truths many times in our lives, but it is only when we are ready for them that they penetrate.

I have described what happened as a shift in understanding. It did not seem like an intellectual experience, and yet I suddenly understood why St. Thomas Aquinas, having devoted his life and considerable intellectual powers to setting down, in his *Summa Theologica,* the entire corpus of Christian teaching, using Aristotelian language of superb clarity, should have described what he had written as "so much straw." I had admired Aquinas since I'd first dipped into the *Summa* as a teenager. Here was a Christian of intellectual distinction who taught that we could come to an understanding of the most important truth, the existence of God, through the unaided use of human reason. We did not have to sit around waiting to be zapped—we could think our way there.

I had been thinking and reading hard for forty years, slowly amassing knowledge but not advancing in understanding. That morning, in the woods outside the Chapel of the Holy Trinity, a door opened. I realized that to approach Christianity, as I had tried, from what seemed to be the logical first step—that is, by examining the arguments for the existence of God—was to tackle it from the wrong end. The most basic principle of learning is to start with the known and move to the unknown. I had been trying to start from the unknowable. Father Amphilochios was proposing that the journey to Christian truth should start with the human experience of love: it should move, that is, from the known to the unknown.

Soon after this conversation, Father Amphilochios told me that he wanted to learn English. This was surprising to me, because his whole life was so wrapped up in the Church and the people of Patmos that he never had time to meet outsiders. Every hour of his day was taken up by teaching, conducting services or being consulted by the islanders. But he asked if I would give him lessons. I was in his debt and found the experience of being with him rewarding, albeit in a rather unsettling way. It was like spending time with somebody from another planet. The things he took pleasure in, the things he was concerned about and, even more important, the things he found trivial were completely at odds with the priorities that had surrounded me for fifty years.

So I was delighted to create with him a schedule which involved my climbing up to his cell at the monastery every Tuesday and Thursday afternoon at five for a half hour's tuition. But I proved a failure as a teacher. Each time I arrived,

Father Amphilochios would insist that we have coffee first, and I would sit on the narrow bed while he lit the tiny gas ring that stood on a wooden crate in the corner of his cell. The coffee demanded attention. He would put about a cupful of water into a long-handled brass coffeepot that was so small it would hold only that much. He then watched it carefully, and as soon as it started to boil he immediately added two teaspoons of ground coffee. This sat on the surface of the water until he added two teaspoons of sugar, at which point the water sank down and went off the boil. After a few seconds it started to rise again, and froth formed. Then he took the pot away from the flame and let the froth sink down, after which he put it back on the heat and stirred vigorously to form another thick froth before pouring it into two cups the size of eggcups. There would be a layer of grounds at the bottom and froth at the top, and very little coffee. And as it was served at boiling point, we had to wait for it to cool before sipping. I describe the process in detail because I sat and observed it each time I arrived at the cell with my notes on easy phrases in English that might be of use to a Greek monk.

Father Amphilochios did not say very much, but tackled the business of preparing the coffee as if he were engaged in a particularly delicate phase of brain surgery: it had his complete attention. Then he would usually suggest that we share a cucumber and would set about the business of peeling it, with the same concentration. This was the exact opposite of what I'd expected. I knew that the monks spent a lot of time meditating and reciting the Jesus prayer and thought he would be far too spiritually rarefied to be domestically competent. I was to learn that the Orthodox sees work as a form of prayer, provided that it is done with concentration and love.

As we ate the cucumber he would ask me, in a mixture of Greek and French, how we were settling in, how we were enjoying Patmos, what the latest problems in the house were, how the children were in England and if it was still raining over there. And by the time we had exchanged our news the half hour was over and the lesson not started. He would apologize and say how much he looked forward to our next meeting.

After a couple of weeks of this, I slowly realized that he had no particular wish to learn English and that the lessons were a pretext. His strategy was simply that we should spend time together. He wanted me to see things differently but was discerning enough to realize that this could not be achieved through argument or discussion. Faith comes through grace; and grace operates most effectively through people—but always through what they are, and not what they say.

There was no doubting the essential goodness of Father Amphilochios. I was moved by it, and perhaps a little changed by it each time I met him. But I was still skeptical about the truth of the faith which inspired that goodness. Historical Christianity was, after all, based on the flimsy and inconsistent records of four Gospels which had been written at least a generation after the events they recorded and as frankly propagandist tracts. The fourth Gospel, of St. John, which I had always enjoyed as poetry, rather like an Arthurian legend or a Norse saga, was written almost a century after the death of Jesus Christ and was acknowledged by scholars to be no more than a beautifully crafted mystical meditation on his teachings. Because I knew it

rather well, I began to use it as a learning aid for my Greek, trying to read passages in the original which I could vaguely remember in English and then checking up doubtful meanings
in a dictionary.

Very soon an amazing thing happened: I came across passages that had no business in a carefully crafted and mystical
meditation. They were little scraps of narrative, oddities that
were irrelevant to the story and sometimes held up the flow of
the drama in a crude and unskillful way. Why, for example,
when building up the tension for the greatest showstopper of
all time—the raising of Lazarus—does St. John bother to tell
us that when Jesus was approaching Bethany, Martha alone
went out to meet him, leaving Mary in the house? And how does
it fit into the mystical meditation that is the tale of the Samari-
tan woman by the well to add that as she rushed off to tell the
people that she had met the Messiah, she left her water bucket
behind?

The final scenes of the trial and execution of Jesus are high
drama and powerfully told, but St. John would have to have
borrowed a film technique from two thousand years in the
future to turn aside and witness the little scene of the servants
in the courtyard warming themselves by a charcoal fire. And
finally, at the climax of the resurrection story, when the empty
tomb is finally revealed in all its awesome significance, why does
St. John, the great mystic, bother to tell us that both Peter and
John ran toward the place and that John got there first but
waited outside until Peter caught up? Then the supremely irrelevant coda: the napkin. At the very moment the first witnesses
are thunderstruck that the prophecies which Jesus made about

his death and resurrection have indeed come true, do we need to be told that the napkin which had covered his face was not lying with the rest of the linen cloths, but rolled up in a different place?

These details—the water bucket, the charcoal fire, the napkin—are not the stuff of mystical allegory. They are the small irrelevancies that hang about in the memory of someone who was present. They do not, of course, prove the truth of the stories. The eyewitness could have lapses of memory; the tales could be embellished to further the propaganda message. But there would be no point in inventing details which do not enhance the propaganda and hold up the pace of the narrative. I began to read St. John again as a story told by a man who was there.

Patmos is the place to read St. John's Gospel, and not just because he once walked here. His imagery is full of light, and although the special quality of light on the island seemed to me one of clarity, Felicia pointed out one morning as we looked across the sunlit valley that here the light does not seem to simply fall on objects—it infuses them and makes them radiant: as if it were giving them life; as if the life and the light were one.

But there is a danger in reading St. John on Patmos. It is that the surroundings, the atmosphere and finally the people might come to persuade you that he speaks the truth. Secure in the post-Christian rationalism of the West, we can enjoy his flights of spiritual imagery as colorful and poetic indulgences from an age before science. But when you live amongst people who have not rejected the spiritual dimension in their lives, his words are sharper: they point not to fantasy but to reality. Every day there is the risk of coming across a situation that reminds you of this. I remember one of the first.

We had started the habit of taking a walk around the island every evening after dinner. I say "around the island," but in fact the walk was just a round-trip of a mile and a quarter from our house, through the village along a circular path that skirted the monastery, and back home. We always stopped in the main square and sat on a little wall by the church to take in the scene at the two restaurants. In summer the tables in the square were always crowded. One of our games each evening was to guess the nationalities from their body language at table: the English always crumpled and apologetic, the Germans spilling out all over and loud, the Italians' arms flailing and theatrical, the French rather taut and disapproving, knowing exactly what they wanted and not ever quite getting it . . .

One evening—it was on the fourteenth of August—we met on our walk Vassos, who collected the town rubbish with a string of donkeys. He was, unusually, sitting at a table on the street, drinking ouzo. Even more unusually, he had a smartly pressed blue shirt and an unfamiliar newly shaved look. I asked him why the party suit and he told me he was on his way to the Monastery of Diasozousa for the night service before the big Festival of the Dormition the following day. Felicia and I decided to look in, even though I have a horror of church festivals. They are always crowded with women in the finest of their finery—an unnerving sight on Patmos, where the finery takes the form of jackets with shoulders like Al Capone's, handbags with yards of brass chain attached and black high-heeled shoes with enormous bright buckles.

These are social occasions on the island, and it is unthinkable to miss one. And they have always seemed to me to have little to do with faith and more a matter of putting in an appearance. They remind me of the village barn dances back home, when everybody got together for a good chat, the men and women in separate groups. As I have a horror of crowds, I tend to skulk in the shadows and leave it to Felicia to participate. But that evening, as we climbed the steps to the big church strung about with electric lights and saw the hundreds of faces looking up at it, I had a strong feeling that they were there for a common purpose, and that this purpose was more than just sociability.

A long queue of local people was waiting to kiss the wonder-working icon. Not having escaped to the fringes of the crowd, I was pulled in. We shuffled along, and as I chatted with people I knew—the electrician, the grocer, the carpenter, the plumber—I was struck by the fact that these people, practical workingmen with no very obvious religious slant to their lives, were doing something extremely odd. They were all patiently standing there in their best suits waiting to kiss a painting. What was really going on?

I remembered something that Philip Sherrard, an Orthodox writer whom I admired, had written about Western society's having lost its way. Materialism had become the creed of the majority, and it was opposed not by the churches but by those who claimed a vague spiritual allegiance or inkling which they insisted had nothing to do with "organized religion." But Sherrard pointed out that any genuine religious tradition provided for some formal discipline as a means of spiritual realization. He wrote that people who attached themselves to these modern, rather gaseous trends of New Worldism were spiritually inferior to the simple believers who practiced a faith sincerely but with only the slightest knowledge of the metaphysical principles on which it was based.

As we stood in the queue at Diasozousa, I realized that these people, by the simple act of kissing the icon, were rejecting the closed system of materialism in which most people of the West are living today. Even if the act is a formal one, done because everybody does it, to revere an icon is to perform an action which proclaims that the material world is not the end— that there is a spiritual dimension to life which we may not understand and which we may ignore in our daily business of living but which on occasions such as this we can come together and publicly acknowledge. To kiss an icon, to cross oneself, to say *"an theli o Theos"* ("God willing"), however perfunctorily or unthinkingly these actions are performed, is to strike a blow at the closed universe of the materialist.

These dawning realizations are among the risks to which anyone exposed to the influences of Patmos is vulnerable.

Seven

⌒ THOSE WHO DESIRE PEACE

PATMOS IS RETICENT about its beauties. At a distance, the island does not make the heart leap with anticipation like Tahiti or Santoríni. Its shape is not that of a romantic mountaintop rising above the sea. Viewed from a boat there is just a low, irregular heap of land with no very prominent features. Only when you come close do you discover the hidden enchantments of the place.

There is an enfolded quality about the bays and valleys here. Instead of wide sweeping stretches of sand open to the sea and the sky, you find little crescent-shaped beaches, their arms curled inward, isolated from each other. When you climb down into one you feel cut off. And as you walk around the coast you see dozens of similar places, each distinct and separate from the others. Patmos is crammed with special places. Old Hands discover them and then pass them on to each other under vows of secrecy. The quality these places share is that of isolation.

Perhaps that is why Patmos became a place of hermits. St. Christodoulos wrote in the eleventh century: "This island has many quiet, deserted places which are recommended to those who desire peace," and even in his time there were already monks who had permission to spend their weekdays alone in a hermitage, returning to the monastery on weekends for the liturgy.

We walked around the hermitages during that first summer on the island. Even then the smaller places were deserted. Perhaps the urge for solitude is no longer so common among monks; or perhaps, as we were told, no place on Patmos is any longer remote. In the remorseless modernizing fever that has gripped Patmos, more recently fueled by funds from the European Common Market, asphalt roads have been built to the farthest hermitages. They are now easily accessible as picnic sites but useless for isolation. But then, the European Common Market has little interest in hermits.

My own interest was sparked by an object that lies among the rocks on a mountainside to the southwest of our house. In the full light of day it looks like just another rock, but as the rays of the setting sun strike it each evening, its contours seem less irregular and it stands out like a stubby stone pillar jutting from the earth. It is hollow. It was built to hold water. It is the cistern of the ruined hermitage of Theoktistos, a solitary monk who was much loved on Patmos. He was a giant of a man, with an olive complexion, dark eyes, thick eyebrows and a thunderous voice.

His beard reached down to his waist and when he was at work building something, which he usually was, he would divide it into two, plait the halves and tie them behind his neck.

Theoktistos came to Patmos in 1875 and built for himself a series of hermitages, usually by simply enlarging a cave among the rocks. He would never stay in one place for more than a few years. This puzzled me, because I pictured the hermit as someone who settles in solitude somewhere and stays there. This apparent restlessness of Theoktistos did not fit in with his character, and I began to investigate him through papers at the monastery library and conversations with older islanders. When I found the answer, it opened for me a rich field of discovery.

The life that Theoktistos chose to lead was ascetic. He had just one pair of shoes, which he had brought with him from Mount Athos, and he wore these only when he visited the monastery. He worked all day at his building or in his garden, but ate very sparsely. He would only put oil on his food on Saturday and Sunday and his diet was wild greens, boiled cabbage, roasted garlic, fruit and *paximadia* (dried bread). Each Saturday evening, the women from nearby villages would take him figs, almonds and *paximadia*. They would also take him their problems. And as he became locally famous for his advice, more and more people would visit him. He became the local agony aunt. So he had to move.

To me, the most intriguing aspect of this was that the problems he solved were not exclusively or even mainly spiritual ones. They dealt with the price of a goat or a family dispute over a field or a marital quarrel—meaning that people within society were going to somebody who chose to live alone for the solutions to the difficulties they had with each other. And I wondered whether the condition of living alone conferred special insights, even about human relationships. Do the hermits deserve their reputation for wisdom?

Ever since St. Anthony of Egypt, in the third century, took himself off into the "waste howling wilderness" of the desert on the east bank of the Nile and lived for twenty years without seeing a human face, there have been Christians who felt best able to live their faith through renunciation. These have often been opposed by other Christians, who, while admitting that Christ fasted for forty days and forty nights, are quick to point out that his first miracle was to keep the wine flowing at the wedding feast. Early Christians were suspicious of asceticism because it was often the mark of the Gnostic.

The keynote of Gnosticism is the duality of spirit and matter. The world and the flesh are evil. They stand in opposition to God. So the spirit is in bondage to the flesh in this life and the Gnostic's aim is to liberate it through asceticism. The early Christians, in contrast, had the view still stressed in the Orthodox Church, that through the incarnation, God deified matter so that the world and material things could be spirit-bearing and enjoyed as God's creation.

Christians were in a better position to enjoy the material things of life after the conversion of Constantine in 313, when Christianity became a passport to the emperor's favor. The rich and powerful in the Roman Empire tended to be Christian. A hundred years later most of the educated population of the Roman cities were Christian and contrasted themselves with the "pagans"—literally, the village or country dwellers. Legitimate power, wealth, even luxury was no longer thought by Christians to be unchristian.

But there were still those who believed that the kingdom of Christ was not of this world and should be sought in solitude and separation. They lived alone as hermits or in small communities, which developed into monasteries. The pioneer of the communal monastic life was St. Pachomius of Egypt, who founded a monastery at Tabennisi on the upper Nile which became so imitated that by the end of the fourth century the whole area, the Thebaid, had become a monastic state numbering thousands of persons. They attracted the hostility and resentment of their contemporaries and the satirical malice of later historians:

> The Ascetics, who obeyed and abused the rigid precepts of the Gospel, were inspired by savage enthusiasm, which represents man as a criminal and God as a tyrant. They seriously renounced the business and the pleasures of the age; abjured the use of wine, of flesh and of marriage; chastised their body, mortified their affection and embraced a life of misery as the price of eternal happiness. [Gibbon, *Decline and Fall,* Ch. 37]

Edward Gibbon was temperamentally ill at ease with asceticism. As the portraits of him testify, he was fond of fine clothes and good food. He was incapable of understanding a human impulse that might prompt rejection of the pleasures of the flesh in favor of an insubstantial spiritual quest. His indictment of the Desert Fathers, his claim that they embraced misery in this life to assure themselves a comfortable billet in the next, is one which can be applied to many Christians of the puritanical flavor, and deserves an answer. I was to find the answer on Patmos, where hermits were folk heroes.

Although on the face of it, at least nowadays, anybody who leaves the comforts of social living and chooses to settle in a remote cave without visible means of subsistence might seem in need of psychological counseling, the Desert Fathers were, for the most part, an astonishingly balanced and sane group of individuals. Of course, there were the extremists who tried to outdo each other in discomfort and deprivation. Their stories have survived, most famously that of St. Simeon Stylites, who spent thirty-seven years living on the tops of various pillars and earned himself a place in most hostile histories of Christianity. But Simeon, it is not often recorded, was expelled from his monastery for extremism and disliked by his contemporaries among the monks for being vain and extravagant. The more common attitude toward asceticism was that of Isidorus the preacher, who wrote: "If you practice your asceticism according to the rules, be careful, when you are fasting, not to get above yourself. If you find yourself feeling proud of your self-denial, eat meat immediately. It is far better to eat meat than to have inflated ideas about yourself."

The healthy distrust of extremes in asceticism is beautifully illustrated in the story of a visit paid by Macarius, a much-loved Desert Father, to the monks at Tabennisi, the monastery of St. Pachomius. At the time, Tabennisi was famous for the spectacular austerities of its monks. Macarius, who was then very old, dressed himself as a laborer and sought the permission of

Abbot Pachomius to be admitted as a monk. The abbot refused, saying that he was far too old and frail to put up with the severe austerities of the brethren. Macarius pleaded at the gate for seven days, and was finally admitted on the condition that he would be expelled immediately should he find himself unable to put up with the hard life.

There were fourteen hundred brethren in the monastery, and Macarius began to study their different kinds of asceticism. One ate only every evening; another every other day; yet another, thought to be on a higher plane, once in five days. One was greatly respected from his habit of spending the nights standing up and allowing himself to sit down only by day. When the season of Lent began, Macarius collected a heap of moistened palm leaves and quietly stood in a corner plaiting them day and night for the forty days until Easter. He ate no bread and drank no water and remained standing day and night for the whole time.

The brethren were so put out by this heroic asceticism that they petitioned the abbot to get rid of this "bodiless man" whose practices put them to shame. They declared that either he must go or they would. Pachomius discovered the true identity of Macarius and thanked him for giving this lesson to his monks so that they might not become haughty about their own ascetic practices, then asked him to return to his hermitage.

The Desert Fathers, although cut off from human society, developed the most striking insights into human psychology, especially in the areas of pride, vanity and humility. Today we all think we understand these terms and can as easily recognize the first two—which are for us synonymous—in others as we do the last in ourselves. But for the Fathers, vanity was simply the desire for the praise of others, whereas pride was subtler and more dangerous. The latter could make a person indifferent to the impression he makes on others. It lurked in the soul and betrayed itself with that first twinge of self-satisfaction that follows a good deed. A brother had lived for many years outside the village where he was born without ever visiting it. One day he said to another brother: "I haven't been to the village for years, but you—you're always going there." When this exchange was related to Abba Poemen, he said, "Me, I'd have dashed over there at night and walked all over the place rather than let myself feel proud for not going there."

Humility, as we have been educated to understand it, means simply having the good manners not to make our superiority in achievement, education or income evident; in this way we avoid causing embarrassment to those less fortunate. We admire those who excel and remain ordinary. The more pious of those who do not excel can comfort themselves by seeing virtue in thinking themselves less than the dust. The Desert Fathers rejected the cant that religious people often attach to humility; humility to the Fathers was simply the rejection of self-centeredness. It was, and is, a powerful means of getting right with the world.

And it was, to the Fathers, the only sure proof against the wiles of the devil. Whenever a monk was making spiritual progress, the devil would intervene. If he was fasting on half a loaf a day, the devil would put in his mind the idea that God would be even more pleased if he could cut it down to half a loaf every two days. The monk who did this and felt any satisfaction in doing so was on the slippery slope. A delightful story illustrates the power of humility. There was a simple brother who had lived alone in the desert for many years in great holiness. One day, Satan decided something had to be done about him, so he disguised himself as an angel and burst into the cell in a blaze of light, announcing: "I am Gabriel, sent from God to declare His delight in you!" The monk glanced up from his plaiting and said simply: "Sorry, you must have the wrong man." Satan vanished.

Humility could be so ingrained as to make it impossible for the monks to behave as other men. There is a pleasant story of a couple of hermits who tried to do so:

> Two brothers had lived together for many years and never had a quarrel. One day, the first said: "Let's have a quarrel like men in the world outside do." The second replied: "But I don't know how to have a quarrel." So the first said: "Look, I'll put down a brick between us and I'll say, 'It's mine.' Then you must say, 'No, it's mine.' And so the quarrel will begin." So they found a brick and put it between them and the first said: "It's mine." And the second said: "No, it's mine." So the first replied: "Oh well, if it's yours, take it." And they did not succeed in having a quarrel.

But the quality most cherished by the Desert Fathers was that of διακρεσις—discrimination or discernment. Without it, practices which were in themselves good could be carried to excess and become harmful. It sees the humorous side of exaggeration and affectation; it deflates pomposity. There is a story from Mount Sinai of a pious brother who called at the monastery there and, seeing the other brothers at work, quoted loftily to the abbot, "Do not work for the food which perishes" [John 6:27], and insisted on being given a vacant cell where he could pray and meditate, quoting the Scriptures again: "Mary has chosen the best part" [Luke 10:42]. The abbot left him there all day, and as the ninth hour (when food was served) came round, the pious brother sat with his eyes fixed on the door, waiting to be called to table. When nobody called him, he came out to see the abbot, asking if the brothers did not eat. "Of course," said the abbot, "but you are a very spiritual man and do not need earthly food. We are fleshly and need to eat—that is why we work. But you, like Mary, have chosen the best part and prefer to spend your time in prayer." The pious brother apologized for his display of self-righteousness and the abbot, using his discernment, said: "Surely Mary hath need of Martha, and it is thanks to Martha that Mary is praised. "

The hermits of Patmos were part of this rich cultural tradition of Orthodoxy, which combines humility and spiritual insight. They left few writings, but stories are still told about them. Probably the earliest hermits were the few who settled near the Cave of the Apocalypse. Among these was Joseph Georgirinis, who lived in the cave itself in 1671, then later became archbishop of Samos and wrote a detailed description of Patmos that was published in 1677. He describes a fig tree which grew near his hermitage, "whose fruit naturally show the letters of the word apocalypse."

A little later came the hermits of Petra, surely the most inhospitable site on the island. Petra is a large bare rock about ten meters high and eighty meters in circumference on a spur of sand near Grikou. It is sometimes called "*kalikatsou*," which is said to be a large black bird the shape of the rock. The rock is steep and difficult to climb, but is pitted with signs of human habitation. There are shallow overhangs with shelves carved into them, ovens, pipes to transport water and even, at the very summit, a narrow and shallow well. It is hard to imagine what impulse could have led men to cling to hollows in the great windswept mass of rock. But they had their own church, that of the Virgin of Filassousis, whose remains, including the holy altar, lie beneath the sea at the foot of the rock.

The closest rival to Petra in terms of the sheer hostility of the environment is the tiny stone island of Petrokaravo, between Patmos and Ikaria. The name means "stone ship," and there is a legend that indeed it was once a pirate ship containing forty pirates which was on its way to plunder Patmos when St. Christodoulos, with his prayers, turned the ship to stone and its lifeboats to the rocks that surround it. The island has no water and little vegetation and is surrounded by sheer cliffs that fall 120 meters into the sea. But there are the ruins of an old building, some small cells and a church that testify to the presence of hermits many years ago. Theoktistos lived there for a year in 1902 and nearly died there when prolonged bad weather prevented the little boat that brought him water from landing.

The boat came from another ancient site for hermitages, the valley of Kipos, which lies at the foot of a ravine on the west of

Patmos, facing Ikaria. It is here that the first gardens were established after the foundation of the monastery; *kipos* means "garden." A few monks stayed in the valley to cultivate the garden and established hermitages there. They built, on a slope above the valley, the Church of the Anargyri, or Holy Unmercenaries, named after two doctors, Cosmas and Damien, who refused to accept fees for their services. There are a few cells close to the church. There is also the Church of the Virgin of the Cross, built close to a spring near the beach and, over to the right of the bay, the tiny Church of the Virgin of Kikkou, named after the icon of the Virgin which is a copy of that in the Monastery of Kikkou, Cyprus. The hermits who built and cared for these churches did so in circumstances unusual for Patmos: surrounded by vegetables and with a plentiful supply of water.

There are also hermitages on a few of the tiny offshore islands of Patmos, which are obvious sites for those seeking isolation. Opposite the harbor of Scala is the island of Hiliamodi, which has a church dedicated to St. Pandeleimon, a cell and a windmill. Tradition tells that the island was cultivated by the monks of the Monastery of St. John, who were at the time so holy they could make the crossing to the island by simply spreading their cloaks on the sea. Their virtues, indeed, were such that they were once rewarded by a harvest of one thousand bushels of wheat, which in Greek is *hilia modia*—hence the name of the island.

Between Hiliamodi and Patmos is the tiny island of Loukakia, also called Pilafi because its shape resembles a heaped dish of rice. In a small cave on the northwest face of the island is a church, now ruined, built in honor of St. Luke the Evangelist.

This too was an isolated hermitage, and in memory of those who lived here in solitude an ex-abbot of the monastery, Father Paul, built a church and cells onshore opposite the island. His nephew, Father Antipas, now abbot of the monastery, has enlarged this.

To the north of Loukakia and close to the southern shore of the peninsula of Geranou is the island of Kentronisi, whose name is said to come from the cedars (*kedra*) planted there by hermits in memory of the Cedars of Lebanon. There are still remains on the island of their stone cells, and one of the last hermits known to have lived there was Theoktistos.

Around the northern side of the peninsula is the most photogenic hermitage on Patmos, that of Apollou. Few of the printed guides can resist a photograph of this domed white church with its closely nestled cells and terraced gardens that step down to an enclosed and remote blue bay. One arm of the bay is a narrow jutting pile of rocks that ends in a stone threshing floor, and there are the remains of a windmill close by. It may seem odd that a Christian hermitage should bear the name of an Olympic god, and some have seen here the last memorial to the golden age of classical Greece. But the Apollo who gave his name to this idyllic retreat was a holy monk from Mount Athos. The story of the gradual growth of this hermitage illustrates well the way such things happen on Patmos.

Apollo settled in this deserted place in 1818 and built a cell, where he lived for forty years. He regularly went to the monastery, and was reading the lesson there at a night vigil when a certain Captain Lazarus, who came from his hometown and happened to have stopped overnight in Patmos because of the bad weather, was in church. He was very impressed by the reading and went to visit Apollo at the hermitage to ask if there was anything he needed. Apollo said that he was a monk and a hermit and that therefore he needed nothing. But the captain insisted on building a little church, so he sold the cargo of rice he had on his ship and gave the money to Apollo to build it.

A handsome and very solid stone wall encloses the hermitage. This was the result of an improbable wager. One day the abbot of the monastery came to visit Apollo, bringing a monk with whom he was having a dispute over the meaning of a passage in Scripture. They had decided to put the matter to Apollo for arbitration, as he was known to be an educated man. Apollo suggested that before he gave his judgment, they should have a wager: the loser would build a wall round the hermitage. Tradition does not tell us who lost, but the wall was built.

Apollo died in 1859 with a great reputation for wisdom and piety. He also deserves to be remembered for his Job-like patience, because he spent the last twenty years of his life horribly afflicted by elephantiasis. After him came hermits from Kentronisi who stayed for thirty-five years, and then another great spiritual father, Macarios, came from Samos and settled at Apollou. He was famous for his austerity (he would not allow lamps at the hermitage), his desire for solitude (he would never answer letters, even from his relatives) and his severity (he told the fishermen of Kambos not to fish on Sundays and gave their wives instruction in how to dress). People came to Macarios for confession on foot, by donkey and by boat from as far away as Lipsos and Kalymnos. He died in 1935.

A generation later visitors again began to call at Apollou. Curiosity, and not the desire for confession, drew them. Until the 1980s it could only be reached on foot or by boat. But the picture in the guidebooks proved a strong draw. In the most popular guide to Patmos, published by the monastery in 1967, tourists are advised that at Apollou "you meet almost always . . . a hospitable watchman that will offer you coffee and fruits under the shade of the trees." The hermitage was doomed. A road was built to its gate and eventually tar-sealed. Apollou was no longer a place for solitude. It is now much visited and still beautiful, but empty.

ON PATMOS, I learned from Bishop Kallistos that the monastery, which is physically and culturally dominant on the island, still preserves the teachings of the Desert Fathers in its tradition. And because these teachings have to be approached by individuals with different levels of sympathy and understanding, they are transmitted, in the Orthodox Church, through the elders, the spiritual fathers. These are men or women of spiritual discernment, but no special ordination or appointment, who can see the best approach to the truth for each individual. The earliest spiritual father was St. Antony himself, who returned after his twenty years of complete solitude to give counsel to others. He was so much in demand that thousands of people came from great distances to seek his advice, and his biographer, Athanasius, wrote that he became a physician to all of Egypt.

The most famous spiritual father in literature is Starets Zossima, from *The Brothers Karamazov,* who was based on a well-known hermit, Ambrose, of Optina Monastery, near Moscow. Intellectuals, writers and politicians from the city, including

Tolstoy, made the trip to Optina to consult Ambrose. Dostoyevsky visited him after the sudden death of his youngest son, Alyosha, and was so impressed by the words of comfort he received that he included them in his novel. And in the character of Zossima, Dostoyevsky speaks of the value to the world of those who retire from it:

> Fathers and teachers, what is a monk? Among the educated this word is nowadays uttered with derision by some people and some even use it as a term of abuse. And it is getting worse as time goes on. It is true, alas it is true, that there are many parasites, gluttons, voluptuaries and insolent tramps among the monks. Educated men of the world point this out. "You are idlers and useless members of society," they say. "You live on the labour of others. You are shameless beggars." And yet think of the many meek and humble monks there are, monks who long for solitude and fervent prayer in peace and quiet . . . In their solitude they keep the image of Christ pure and undefiled for the time being, in the purity of God's truth which they received from the Fathers of old, the apostles and martyrs and when the time comes they will reveal it to the wavering righteousness of the world.

I wondered, on Patmos, during that first confrontation with its monasticism, how far those words of Dostoyevsky, written over a hundred years before, might apply here. "And it is getting worse as time goes on," he had written then. The idea that the monastery might be the repository of some pure and undefiled truth must seem remote to the thousands of visitors who crowd its cramped spaces and file past its jeweled miters, ornate silver candelabra, richly enameled reliquaries, gilded silver chalices and gold-embroidered vestments on display in the treasury. They pay to see precious objects on display; it is no part of the organized tour that they should be exposed to anything of more lasting value. And perhaps this is realistic, because most of the tourists do not seem to arrive with a mind-set that suggests they might be sensitive to spiritual promptings.

The summer cruise groups that arrive panting and exhausted at the monastery gate seem emblematic of the "wavering righteousness of the world." The island-hopping has been fun so far but this is duty, and anyway, the price is inclusive. They stub out resentful cigarettes at the door and compose their faces into the glum and comatose masks that seem fitting for a religious building. The women wrap beach towels around their bikinis and the men pull on pajama bottoms over their boxer shorts, but still display the cheery mottoes on their T-shirts. "TAKE ME DRUNK I'M HOME," "KEEP ON FUCKING!" or "WOT AGAIN? YOU MUST BE KIDDING!" accompanied by the outline of a glans penis dripping semen.

These are not worn as protest messages against the monastery. They simply indicate the distance between the tourists and the monks, who as they flit around the monastery courtyard often seem furtive and unavailable. This is possibly because they do not share a common language with the great majority of the visitors, and also because they know that the bikini ladies are keen to be photographed with them. I saw one snarl and brush aside a camera pointed at him. But then, perhaps the T-shirts had driven him beyond endurance.

The monastery has been, for centuries, the focus of controversy on the island. In the past it was all-powerful, owning the land and governing the lives of the islanders. In our own time its influence has shrunk to the point that travel agents can be heard claiming that they and not the abbot are in charge of opening times. They, after all, ferry the tourists by the thousands up the hill to the monastery gate from waiting cruise ships, then pass on part of the proceeds to the monastery coffers. It is a profitable business and, for the monastery, the overhead is low.

But the disturbance is great. The delicate atmosphere of tranquillity and prayer does not survive the mass invasion of those who are out of sympathy with it. Silence is always defeated by noise. And there are many who call for the visitors to be controlled, their numbers cut or even restricted to the Orthodox only. I have talked about this often both with travel agents and monks. To my surprise, the senior monks have a tolerance which is based not on resignation, but on their faith. The monastery is indeed, they say, a place of prayer, a focus for the faith. And, however preoccupied or unsympathetic the visitors may seem en masse, there is always the possibility that one or two may be open to the Truth which the monastery exists to preserve and celebrate. For the sake of those few, it must remain open to the many.

Eight

➣ FROM ANOTHER COUNTRY

WE WERE RIDING the old Yamaha motorbike up the hill to Chora one day, Felicia on the pillion seat and the shopping in an orange box strapped onto the back mudguard, when a car nosed past. It was a shining metallic-blue Mercedes coupe, encasing an immaculate couple who looked relaxed and at ease with the world, as people in expensive cars so often do. The sight triggered a sudden realization in both of us. Without having adopted a new philosophy or even making a conscious decision to change our status, we had become downsizers.

I was never a television personality in Britain, not in the sense of being a national household name. But because I appeared on the BBC's major channel once a week for the better part of ten years, people sometimes recognized my face. Most of them could not put a name to it. This may not seem like a problem, not compared with that of real stars. I was never mobbed in the street, never had the shirt ripped off my back by teenage girls inflamed with lust. I was never asked to lay a foundation stone or start a marathon.

But to be almost known can be scarier than to be well known. People would stare at me in supermarket queues and nudge their partners and whisper, almost always getting back a shake of the head or shrugged shoulders. Sometimes they would call "Hi!" in the street and then pause, frown and turn their eyes to one side. I was once hailed by a drunk who soon became abusive because I didn't throw my arms round him. He knew me well. He had seen me regularly in his home. Why the hell was I all unfriendly?

The BBC has a worldwide reputation for parsimony. Its attitude is that if you get the chance to make programs there you have been allowed to join an exclusive band of the especially talented and should not expect to get paid as well. Fortunately for me, Felicia operated as my agent and was able to screw modest fees out of the corporation so that we could eat. In fact, for about ten years we ate, it must be said, rather well.

I ran a metallic-blue Mercedes coupe with the *Good Food Guide* always in the glove compartment. I bought the car because a television reporter had told me how important it was to be able to jump straight out of a car after a long trip and present yourself to camera looking neat, bright and energetic. Our Subaru farm truck always delivered me dusty and crumpled, so I decided to invest in a little Germanic technical wizardry and bought the Merc. The television reporter was right: it always de-livered me fresh. But that may have been because it never took me very far. Most of the engine components were under the control of computer chips that would occasionally close every-thing down and bring me smoothly to a halt after a few miles in the English countryside. The mechanics who live in such places are not experienced in Germanic technical wizardry but never like to admit this. So they would lift the hood, nod slowly, suck their teeth and order a tow truck. Driving a Mercedes coupe is, I can report, a restful experience, especially if you are being towed.

The *Good Food Guide* governed our eating. We would drive for miles, usually in the Subaru farm truck, to any res-taurant that had collected a few stars. We often returned home by taxi. This was because I had decided that no meal should start without a couple of pink gins; the fish course had to have a decent Chablis; meat was unthinkable without a château-bottled claret; whatever the pudding, it was improved by a Beaumes-de-Venise; and the finest *digestif* in the world was a really decent bottle of champagne. Felicia would do her part in helping me put away this load of alcohol—mainly, I sus-pect, to protect me from drinking it all myself—and we would be driven home, speechless.

It was a taxing life. Making television programs on loca-tion is like warfare: hours of boredom followed by seconds of panic. Like the time I had to speak a piece to camera about the pope from a tiny hotel veranda in some small Italian town. His Holiness was due to walk down the street below at some time during the morning and the cameraman had worked out that he would be in shot over my shoulder for about eight seconds. I had to speak the piece as he passed. If I stumbled over a word I couldn't shout down to him to go back and walk it again. You can deliver twenty-five words in eight seconds. That means twenty-five chances to slip up. And then, of course, there's the sun to worry about: will it slip behind a cloud and plunge the scene into darkness when you're halfway through? Will the focus-puller on the camera get it right? Will the battery on the radio mike hold up? Will some drunk in the crowd shout "Viva il Papa" when I'm halfway through? And, of course, the important thing is to look relaxed.

But it wasn't the tensions of life in front of the camera that drove me to give it up—it was the claim that television makes on your life. When you are making a film, that film becomes the focus of your existence. The production team of producer, director, researchers, editor—and me—eat, breathe and sleep the film until it is finished. Because there is never enough time and there are always unforeseen crises, we often had to give up food and sleep to get the job done. But then the perverted notion crept in that the film would not be any good *unless* we had given up both food and sleep in the making of it. At this stage I began to suspect that I was in the wrong job.

It seems amazing now that it took me so long to realize this. I knew that my happiest times were when I was at home with Felicia. But the job I had chosen kept me traveling around the world, spending my nights alone in a king-sized bed at some Holiday Inn after working my way through the overpriced contents of the minibar. When I got home it was for a quick change of clothes and the swapping of stories at a superficial level—I was too emotionally exhausted to talk about anything that really mattered—before I was off again.

WHEN WE FIRST BOUGHT THE HOUSE IN GREECE, there seemed no reason why we should not keep up the high living during the winters. Much of the television studio work is done in that season and I had plenty of offers to do voice-overs for television films, which is undemanding and well paid. We were confident that the comfortable lifestyle we had created would continue.

But after the first summer on Patmos the work dried up. This was partly because the most important qualification for appearing on television is that you appear on television. I had been off the screen for six months and producers, many of whom had not had their jobs for that long, were beginning to ask, "Peter who?" The voice-over bookings ceased when the agents who tried to make them finally gave up trying to persuade our neighbor in Chora, who spoke no English, to run across the street and call us to her phone. (We could not get our own phone, for reasons that I shall go into later). So people offering me employment had to make the simple choice between learning Greek, if they wanted me, or giving the job to somebody else.

When the income shrinks there are two alternatives: work harder to increase it, or reduce your expenditures. Thus it was that in my mid-fifties, I decided that hard work is overrated. So we scaled down. The *Good Food Guide* restaurants were not hard to give up. I should be sad to have missed them, but as a regular experience over the years, they don't come up with many surprises; besides, we both love cooking. I had always followed

Kingsley Amis when it came to drinking, and his advice on wines was that it was far more important that they be plentiful than that they be of high quality. We gave up the château-bottled clarets and began to buy flagons of what the Australians amiably call Red Ned. Clothes, for someone no longer in the public eye, had to be decent but did not need to give off any messages. I decided that I had come by enough during my television years to see me out.

Patmos is encouraging to the downsizer. This is firstly because conspicuous consumption is not fashionable here. Even the international jet set cast aside their finery when they come to Patmos and walk around town like everybody else in T-shirts and shorts. Occasionally their guests will slip up and turn out in something eye-catchingly expensive, but they very soon catch on to the general mode and begin to dress down. When a visiting skin diver from New York tried to explain away his solid gold Rolex Oyster on the grounds that he used it for stunning sharks in the Caribbean, he was told that he might at least have the decency not to wear it in public.

Downsizing comes easier in a society with such attitudes. Shortly after we arrived, an unknown English couple knowing very little Greek, doing our own housework and snapping up any bargains on offer at the shops, the Patmians quickly got our measure.

A lot of romantic gush has been written about the joys of the simple life. Fortunately it has no effect on the purchasing public, or Western society would suffer economic collapse, since its prosperity depends on people buying things they don't need. Over the years, efficient marketing techniques have implanted the "must have" notion in the psyches of younger and younger people. And this keeps the wheels of industry spinning to turn out trendy trainers or Japanese computer games and so on, to the increase of general prosperity. We did not downsize as a gesture of protest against consumer society. We simply found ourselves with a reduced income and set about discovering the things we could do without.

We were helped by situating ourselves in a place where it is quite difficult to spend money in the ways we spent it before. Patmos did not have available the range of goods that eat up income at an expanding rate so that you never feel you have quite enough. And doing without them has the therapeutic effect of slowing you down. It takes time to hand-wash clothes or to jump up and down on sheets, rinse them, wring them out and hang them on a line between trees in the garden; to top and tail the beans; to mix, whip and grate by hand; to haul up buckets from a well. A life without gadgets develops a different, slower rhythm. And, oddly, more time seems to be available in a life without labor-saving devices.

Living abroad changes you. There is, first of all, the continual learning process of coming up against local people who are different, who see the world through different eyes and respond to it in ways that have been shaped through generations of different conditioning. Then there is the experience of meeting people who are also abroad and whose behavior, on that account, is changed.

It took a while to learn about ways in which Patmians see life differently from us; ordinary social encounters tend to bring to the fore the things people share. And we had lived abroad long enough to avoid slipping into those easy generalizations about another culture that are the weakness of the expatriate. But we found ourselves committing enough social gaffes in our early months to realize that a few broad notions of how Patmians tend to behave could come in handy.

For example, "How are you?" in England is not a request for information about a person's health; it is just a cheery noise we make when we meet each other, and expects no more than a return: "Fine, how are you?" which is not a question either. On Patmos, if you ask how someone is, you are likely to be told—to the last arthritic twinge in the precisely located joint. You will hear how long the current indisposition has been around, which members of the family suffer from it, what measures have been recommended by which doctors, how effective/futile they have been, how much they cost, whether, or how many times, the ultimate step has been taken: *enesi* (injection).

Patmos was for many years a medical backwater—or perhaps it would be nearer the truth to say a proving ground. The town hall still bears the legend on its face in its reference to "AGROTIKI YATREION," which means "rural or agricultural doctor," indicating that the medical services are in the hands of a recently qualified physician doing a compulsory period of practice in a remote area before being allowed to start a career in a major center of population. Our earliest ailments were dealt with in a pleasantly informal and democratic way by what in England would be called junior housemen.

Having picked up an ear infection a few weeks after moving in, I went down to the clinic one morning to find a large room whose chairs were all occupied. There were posters on the wall giving information about AIDS, and when I asked a local woman what they said she replied that she didn't know but that it had to do with giving money to the poor. In the middle of the room was a table, at which sat two white-coated young men with stethoscopes. The props were reassuringly authoritative, as neither young man had long needed to use a razor. There were two chairs opposite the doctors, into which we moved as they became vacant. When we announced our disorders, everybody in the room took a keen interest, and the initial diagnosis was arrived at after an exchange of views between the doctors and contributions from the audience.

It was when we got down to the treatment that democracy really swung into action. As the doctors suggested ointments or pills, somebody in the audience would have already used them and found them miraculously therapeutic or a complete waste of money. We'd have a lively exchange, the doctor would scribble a prescription after hearing views on all sides and I'd leave feeling that a broad spectrum on human experience had been brought to bear on my problem. There is a story doing the rounds of the immigrant community on Patmos that the young physicians are sent to the island with only two words of English, which encapsulate the two courses of action appropriate for medical problems on the island, trivial or serious. The words are "aspirin," for cases that can be dealt with on the island, and "helicopter," for the rest.

There is one aspect of living abroad that is rarely mentioned in travel books and completely ignored in the printed guides, even though it often causes more anxiety than any other. It is how to handle financial inducements. Everyone hears that if you expect services in countries around the Mediterranean you have to oil the wheels. This is not, we are told, immoral; it is simply a different way of doing things. But there's a dearth of reliable information on how to set about it. With this in mind, I have decided to be completely frank about our experiences on Patmos.

The Greek word for a bribe is *fakelo,* a euphemism that means literally "envelope" and refers to what it contains. I had my first experience of a *fakelo* transaction when I sought planning permission for some minor alteration on the house. A *fakelo* would be necessary, I was told by the Old Hands; it was expected and part of the normal way of doing things on the island. So I sought advice on how I should hand it over. Do you wait till after sunset and accost the appropriate official in a dark alley? Do you hand it to him in the office in broad daylight with a grin and a wink? Or do you send it through the mail?

I was lucky to have experienced advisers who gave me the whole script. I should go to the official's house on a Saturday morning, taking the planning application and the *fakelo.* I should explain that I needed to make this application but that my Greek was not up to filling in the form. I should ask his help and then, when the form was completed, hand it back to him with the *fakelo,* which I should explain contained a little something for his trouble.

I was very nervous as I knocked on the door that Saturday morning, carrying an empty planning application and a brown envelope containing twenty thousand drachmas, the amount specified to me by the Old Hands. I had never tried to bribe anybody before, and even though everyone had told me that this was perfectly normal and the way things were done on Patmos, I was terrified that a passing policeman might notice the *fakelo* and run me in. And then I should have to set about bribing *him*. The possibility of being drawn into an endless web of corruption was starting to produce nausea.

But all went surprisingly well. The official was at home and glad to help. His wife made me a cup of coffee and we filled in the form together: I supplied the answers and he wrote them down. When we finished I got up, shook his hand and turned to leave. The *fakelo* was lying mute on the table and no mention had been made of it. I opened the door with a great sense of relief and stepped outside.

Then he handed me the *fakelo*. "You forgot this," he said. "Oh no, that's for you—just a little something for your trouble . . ." "But it's no trouble. I like to help you." "Well, it's Saturday morning, your free day, and I've come bothering you at home . . ." I was beginning to get desperate. "Nothing at all!" he said emphatically, pushing the envelope into my hand. I knew I was failing. Then, inspiration: "Would you post my application for me please?" I said. "When the post office opens on Monday? To save me the trip down to Scala?" He shrugged and nodded, smiling. So I thrust the *fakelo* into his shirt pocket and babbled, "Then that's for the postage," as I rushed out the door.

He did not follow. I marched down the street with a spring of triumph in my step. It had worked! I was a man of the world. I could pass a bribe with the best of them. No more problems with bureaucracy for us. Now I knew how to smooth out the wrinkles. For the rest of that weekend I walked tall.

That Monday morning I was riding the motor scooter down the hill to Scala when I saw the official riding up in the opposite direction. He waved at me to stop and handed me my *fakelo*. "I posted the application for you," he said. "Here's the change." Then he rode off. I opened the envelope. Inside were 18,850 drachmas. The stamp had cost 150 drachmas. I had failed. I never tried again. I have decided that bribery on Patmos is like sex: there is far more talk than action.

Gradually, during that first summer on Patmos, we came to know more about the way of life of our neighbors. And they, of course, learned about us. There was plenty of room for misunderstanding. We quickly fell into a routine of breakfasting on the veranda and then working for the rest of the morning. I was writing a book and Felicia would paint. Because I wrote in the corner of our bedroom, I would duck back in there once I'd finished washing up. We heard after some weeks that our neighbors thought this very odd: "They get up, have breakfast and then go straight back to bed for the rest of the day."

We were living close to Marouso, her sister and her mother. Their houses were literally a stone's throw apart, and they had many friends living close by. Each house had a small veranda on the south side, and it was from these platforms that the daily chats were conducted. I had often wondered why Byzantine singers tilt back their heads and produce a strangulated wail not at all easy on Western ears. Of course, it is to produce a strident tone that can be heard in the vast spaces of a Byzantine church. This is exactly the technique used by our neighbors in exchanging news and views across the rooftops that separated their verandas. It was alarming at first because we had thought that only a life-threatening situation could produce such sounds from a human throat; but we got used to it. We called it the Patmos telephone.

The more conventional telephones that operate down wires were hard to come by. At the office of OTE, the telephone company, there was a thick book of lined paper containing the names of people who had applied for telephones to be installed, arranged in the order of their applications. As the weeks rolled by, engineers would slowly work through the list. But what with the interruptions of repairs, annual holidays, sickness, strikes and saints' days, progress was slow. We were told that an established way of jumping the queue was to have oneself certified as suffering from a serious heart condition likely to require immediate medical assistance. We were even given the name of a doctor in Athens who would, for a *fakelo,* supply the necessary certificates. Another shortcut was to buy a telephone number from somebody who was leaving the island. But we found it relaxing to be cut off for a time and decided to take the step which nobody recommended: wait our turn. At the beginning and end of each season I'd call in at the OTE office to be shown the book of hopefuls and congratulated on our gradual ascent toward the top of the list. After three years we got our phone.

A note here on the importance of waiting may be appropriate. There are certain procedures that are felt in Greece to be of such gravity and moment in our lives that it would be indecent to hurry them. The acquisition of a telephone is one. So is the issuance of an annual motorcycle licence. This procedure involves waiting in a queue at the police station for a form; taking the form to a bookshop, where you buy stamps; sticking the stamps on the form until it is filled in; then taking it back to the police station and exchanging it for another form, which itself has to be carefully filled in by pressing with a ballpoint pen through several layers interleaved with carbon paper. The philosophy behind this structure of impediments to indecent haste was neatly and economically expressed in the reply which friends of ours received to their request for a decision on a planning application: they had "not been waiting long enough."

Hospitality across cultures is not easy to get right. We soon found out that if somebody buys you a carafe of wine in a restaurant it is inept to send one immediately back. In England a careful watch is kept on whose turn it is to buy a round of drinks, and the man who "misses his shout" is soon the outsider. But in Greece overanxiety to repay a social debt is seen as a sort of ingratitude. This is not to say that obligations can be ignored, just that they must be settled after a decent interval.

It is easier, we found, to get used to the different foods eaten on Patmos than to the hours at which Patmians eat. The chief of police, whose wife spoke English and shared with Felicia an interest in painting, asked us out to dinner once in the early days. I felt flattered to be noticed by such a distinguished and powerful man, and might even have enjoyed the occasion if it had not begun at 10:15 P.M. He came off duty, he explained, at 10 P.M., and so could start to relax with us a quarter of an hour later. But we were usually in bed by then, usually having eaten a couple of hours earlier, and the evening was a struggle to stay awake followed by hours of indigestion. Locals usually get together for dinner when we have been long asleep. And they usually bring the children.

There is on Patmos a relaxed attitude toward time, which can be either therapeutic or frustrating. It amounts to a refusal to be controlled by the tyranny of the clock. Appointments tend to be made *to proi* (in the morning), *to apoyevma* (in the late afternoon) or *to vrathi* (in the evening). If a foreigner's anal anxieties are such as to call for a specific hour, then that will be smilingly agreed to; but when the hour comes and passes and the appointment is not kept this is felt to be the natural order of things, calling for no explanation or excuse. The blackboard on the stern of the *kaiki* may say that it will leave at 10 A.M. but if at that time it is only half-full, then everyone waits till other passengers arrive.

This flexible attitude toward arrangements of all kinds is relaxing for those who are temperamentally attuned to flow along with the stream of life. It is not anarchic: there is nothing subversive or deliberate in the unpunctuality. It is not even conscious. One of the younger monks, some years ago, came up with the idea of having a monastery information center. He asked if I would help set it up, do the translations and put in a few hours every day. Many pilgrims, he realized, could not find out details about what church services were available, where they took place and what hours they started, and it would be a great help to these people to distribute a timetable giving such details. The abbot had agreed to give us a room close to the monastery steps.

We could furnish it with books, a couple of armchairs and a gas ring for making coffee. There we could entertain pilgrims, answer their questions and distribute our timetables.

I congratulated him on being in tune with the age of information and told him I would be delighted to help. But I sensed one possible flaw. I could not remember the number of times I had crawled out of bed at dawn to walk over a mountain track so as to arrive at a particular church in time for its feast day, only to find nobody there. This was often because a number of churches shared a feast day and so some of them would have to celebrate a day late. Nobody quite knew who would celebrate when until the last minute. It was not unknown for us to turn up for a Sunday liturgy at our local monastery to find the doors barred, the priest having gone to Athens or been called on to perform other duties at the big monastery. And we had learned that the feast day of our nearest church could happen over a range of days and that, although vespers was said to begin at 5 P.M., it rarely got under way before 6:30.

So the problem with the monastery information center project was determining where we should go to get the correct information. There was never a lack of information, simply no means of checking up on its accuracy. I felt that it was better, if only marginally, to have no timetable than to put our efforts into distributing one that was inaccurate. The project lapsed.

IT SEEMED TO US that anybody who chooses to settle in a foreign country has to decide which local habits to adopt and which to reject. We had seen the British who try to "go native" as well as those who become caricatures of Englishness when confronted by an alien culture: dressing for dinner and importing their food. We settled somewhere in the middle, eating the local produce but doing so at hours with which our metabolisms could cope.

Anybody who is not born and bred on Patmos is a *xenos,* a word that the dictionary translates as "foreigner," "alien," "stranger" or "guest." And the word is indeed used today with all those importantly different meanings. Romantically inclined guidebooks, especially those published fifty years ago, stress that, to the Greeks, any stranger is a guest to whom is owed a duty of hospitality. Within the Orthodox tradition, the duty of entertaining strangers lives on, with its attendant possibility of entertaining angels unawares.

One of the most popular icons is the *Hospitality of Abraham,* of which there is a beautiful twelfth-century fresco in the Chapel of the Virgin at the Monastery of St. John. This depicts the story told in Genesis 18 in which three strangers suddenly appear before Abraham by the oaks of Mamre as he is sitting at the door of his tent in the heat of the day. Abraham immediately calls for water to wash their feet and has a meal prepared for them. In Orthodox tradition, this is held up to be the proper treatment of strangers.

So the tradition of instant and unquestioning hospitality to the *xenos* is ancient and strong. It still exists in remoter parts of the island, and I have been stopped by a goatherd while walking alone in the hills and pressed to share a cucumber or to drink a cup of water. But in recent years strangers have been arriving here at the rate of several thousand a day in the high season, and this puts pressure on spontaneous hospitality. It also alters the ways in which Patmians think of the *xenos*. Instead of the vulnerable wanderer far from home and probably hungry or thirsty, today's *xenos* has probably just stepped off a luxury cruise liner with a bulging paunch and wallet looking for something to buy ashore in the short time available and is wary of being cheated.

So, of course, the word *xenos* no longer awakens in Greeks the protective instinct toward a guest to whom unstinting hospitality is due. Here on Patmos it tends to mean a stranger who is on holiday with time to spare and money to spend. It helps to remember this when we stand with English deference in a queue at the post office or bank and find a local pushing to the front and demanding service. We are, after all, *xenoi:* we can't be about anything very serious. We can wait.

Although the *xenos* on Patmos can cover anybody from a visiting Athenian to a package tourist from Detroit, the foreigners on the island tend to fall into distinct groups who have little contact with each other. Chora is on the circuit for an international group, many of whom have bought and refurbished and even rebuilt the grander houses, who come here for a couple of weeks or so once a year to see each other in a different context. The rest of us know they have arrived when we see house servants in the streets taking pet dogs for walks.

They arouse the envy and animosity which is the natural response to affluence, and it is often said that local people are resentful of them because they have driven up the price of houses in Chora to the point where only the rich foreigners can afford to live in them. The truth is that most of the really large houses would not be suitable for anybody but the really well-off. The cost of repairing and rebuilding them under the careful eye and with the advice and consent of the Archaeological Department would be far beyond what most Patmians could afford or would be prepared to pay. So the mansions of Chora, built by the affluent, remain, in their reconstructed form, in their hands.

The status of *xenos* has its obvious disadvantages. It is easy to feel slighted, put upon, even abused by the locals, often when no discourtesy is intended. When, as often happens on Patmos, things don't work out as expected or even promised, we can feel personally slighted, although very few things here ever do work out as expected or even promised. The health-conscious *xenos* worries about island medical services and could not have been reassured by a recent rumor that the local doctors did not know how to read their new equipment for testing blood pressure and had sent streams of perfectly healthy Patmians off to Athens for bypass surgery. And when caught up in the labyrinth of Greek bureaucracy, a *xenos* is hard-pressed to avoid the feeling that the anfractuosities form part of a personal attack and cannot be the way things are regularly done.

But there are compensations to being a *xenos*. It is very easy, for example, to escape baleful social situations by protesting that you did not understand the invitation. Your absence at Tuesday evening's drinks party will be excused at least partly when you admit that you can't yet distinguish with confidence between the Greek words for "Tuesday" and "Thursday." If you behave oddly, the chances are that people may think this is the way you do things back home: your conduct will be put down to your nationality, which is bad for international relations but lets you off the hook.

Above all the status of *xenos* is a privileged one, for it lets you see things with new eyes. Because so much is unfamiliar, you are like a child learning about the world. Impressions are strong and moving. To be a *xenos* is to be open again to surprise and wonder.

Nine

⁀ More Enduring Than Gold

Living in a place not only changes your awareness of the present; it can completely alter your view of the past. The version of history attaching to a place that seems entirely plausible on the printed page can just fail to ring true when you are on the scene. As we found in the case of the eminent traveler and Cambridge scholar Dr. Edward Daniel Clarke, who visited Patmos in 1801. He returned to the general acclaim of his fellow scholars, was appointed university librarian and had a monument erected to his memory in the chapel of Jesus College in honor of his services to scholarship. His own account of his adventures on Patmos and his rescue of priceless gems of literature from ignorance and squalor was published to considerable praise in 1812. It makes lively reading.

It was at eight-thirty on an early October morning in 1801, runs the story, when the skiff *Arethusa* swung into view outside the harbor of Scala and headed for port. The vessel was carrying Edward Clarke on a mission of scholarly redemption: to rescue whatever valuable books and manuscripts he could find from their inevitable destruction at the hands of the monks of Patmos. His little boat made a strange spectacle at the time, because it was displaying an ensign almost as big as itself. Before entering the harbor at Patmos, Clarke had decided to run up the English flag. This was a gift from his brother, a naval captain, who had suggested to him that it would be a good idea to hoist it when nearing land, not so much to impress the locals as to stop them from firing on the boat as a pirate ship.

Suddenly a chorus of derisive shouts from local fishing boats wafted across the bay. It seemed that Captain Clarke's flag had failed to inspire awe among the local natives. Perhaps its dimensions, appropriate for a warship of the line, seemed over-assertive to the point of ridicule on a tiny open boat. Clarke was put out. He had not previously encountered aggressive rowdiness among the islanders of the Dodecanese and he felt that his position as an Englishman should attract more respect. Then, as they approached the boats, Clarke saw that the fishermen were not local Greeks. They were wearing the white shirts and shako hats of the French revolutionary army.

Two months earlier, the English army at Alexandria had routed Napoleon's invading force. Ten thousand French troops had set sail from Egypt, and many were still on their way home. Clarke, with his outsize banner, had run into a bunch of the defeated French. "*Voilà un beau venez-y voir!*" they shouted. "*Le pavilion Anglois! Tremblez, messieurs!*" ("Here's a sight worth seeing! The English flag! Gentlemen, tremble!")

They were, wrote Clarke, "much too numerous to venture a reply," and as his party landed they found the quay covered with French soldiers and officers. Things seemed to be turning out awkwardly for the lone Englishman in so remote a place, surrounded as he was by the resentful and undisciplined soldiers of a defeated enemy.

But the French needed his help. They had not left Egypt empty-handed. Along with their own personal property, they were carrying back to France a number of wooden cases bearing the home addresses of their generals. These cases contained Egyptian antiquities for sale to museums and private collectors. The plundering of Egypt had just begun. The first rich pickings lay unprotected on the Patmos waterfront.

The officers made an immediate appeal to Clarke. The stolen treasures of Egypt were attracting attention. The transport ship which they had hired to convey them back home was under the command of an Algerian captain who had twice tried to poison their food so that he could get his hands on the loot. He had insisted on putting in at Patmos under the pretense of needing to careen the vessel, saying that it was unsafe to continue the voyage until this had been done. The officers, fearing that he intended to sail off with the booty once they were onshore, had insisted on off-loading the cases, which were stacked on the quay. They'd posted a guard, but the wine of the island was so plentiful and potent that the soldiers were too drunk every day to be watchful. In desperation, the officers petitioned Clarke to present their case to the British minister at Constantinople and to request that another vessel be sent to Patmos from there or Smyrna to take them home. In the meantime, they had to find a secure building to store the cases.

Clarke was touched by this change of tone from the raucous welcome, which had slightly discomposed him, and he agreed to help. The obvious place of security was the fortified monastery at the top of a mountain behind the port, and he decided to climb up there without delay to intercede with the abbot for the protection of the French and their loot.

The ascent to the monastery was steep and rugged, but Clarke, accompanied by his interpreter, whom he called Mr. Riley, managed to find a couple of donkeys to take them up there. The senior French officer went with them. The superior and the bursar welcomed them in the refectory and Clarke presented to them the letter of authority he was carrying from the Turkish *capudan pasha,* the officer in charge of the Dodecanese; this, being in Turkish, was translated by Mr. Riley. On hearing the letter, the monks agreed to receive the trunks within the monastery walls, and this business being settled, Clarke turned to the main object of his visit, which was to see the library.

He was taken into "a small oblong chamber having a vaulted stone roof," which was nearly filled with books and manuscripts. The ignorant monks, thinking the books (which were of relatively recent vintage) to be the more valuable items, had placed them on shelves around the room. The manuscripts, many of which were irreplaceable and of high antiquity, were heaped up in the middle of the floor, a prey to damp and rats; they were obviously being used by anybody who happened to need an odd piece of parchment. The superior told Clarke that his favorite books were the new ones, "but when we took down one or two of them to examine their contents, we discovered that neither the superior nor his colleagues were able to read." Clarke asked the superior if he knew what was in the pile on the floor, and "he replied, turning up his nose with an expression of indifference and contempt: *Xeirographia* [manuscripts]."

Clarke's sensibilities as a scholar and bibliophile were affronted. He wrote: "It was, indeed, a moment in which a literary traveller might be supposed to doubt the evidence of his senses; for the whole of this condemned heap consisted entirely of Greek Manuscripts, and some of these were of the highest antiquity."

Clarke was in a torment. The appalling waste in front of his eyes dismayed him; but he knew that to show the slightest interest in acquiring any of the material would make it impossible for the monks to agree that he should have it. Fortunately he had the services of his experienced interpreter: "We referred the matter to Mr Riley, as to a person habituated in dealing with knavish Greeks; and presently such a jabbering took place, accompanied with so many significant shrugs, winks, nods and grimaces that it was plain something like a negotiation was going on."

Clarke spent the time rummaging in the heap of manuscripts and discovered there a copy of the twenty-four first dialogues of Plato dating from the ninth century, a lexicon of St. Cyril of Alexandria and two small volumes of psalms and hymns which seemed to have ancient Greek musical notes drawn in. He had also just picked out a tiny volume of Philo's writings on animals when he was stopped by Mr. Riley, who said he had struck a deal with the superior for the purchase of the volumes so far selected, but that the deal might be called off if Clarke asked for more. He said that the sale of the books had to be kept secret from the inhabitants of the town, and hid a couple of the smaller volumes in the folds of his Turkish robe, adding that the two monks would be responsible for sending on the rest of the books.

Clarke had little confidence in the honor of the monks, but realizing there was no alternative, left the most valuable part of his acquisition in very doubtful hands. They were about to leave the library when the French officer returned with the trunks and showed the different approach to negotiating which his nation would have taken: on hearing that Clarke had found many items which he would gladly purchase, the officer burst out: "Purchase! I should never think of purchasing from such a herd of swine: if I saw anything I might require, I should, without ceremony, put it in my pocket and say 'Bonjour.'"

But Clarke could proceed only as his gentler English conscience dictated, and he left the money (an unspecified amount) and most of the books with the two monks, setting off down the donkey track to the port. About halfway down the track, they turned off to the right to inspect the cave where according to local superstition St. John had lived and written the Apocalypse. This cave was disappointing, the claims made for it clearly fraudulent: "It is not spacious enough to have afforded a habitation even for a hermit; and there is not the slightest probability that any thing related concerning it, by the monks, is founded in truth." There seemed to be something like a school being run in a building by the cave, but its superintendent was ill-informed, and Clarke would conclude: "It is hither that the Greek families send their sons to be educated by a set of monks unable to read their own or any other language."

Clarke stayed at Patmos for nearly a week and made another visit to the monastery, hoping to rescue other valuable treasures from the depredations of the monks, but he was frustrated because the local people insisted on going with him. The superior explained that he was personally very willing to sell the manuscripts but that the local people acted as spies for the Turkish *capudan pasha;* if the Turks found out that he was making any money, they would come over and collect it.

On Sunday, October 11, the day on which the abbot had promised to deliver the manuscripts, Clarke and his party saw no one, and toward sunset they began losing hope, especially as Mr. Riley had left them for Constantinople. But then they saw a man approaching the quay with a large basket on his head, making signs that he wanted to be picked up. They sent over a little skiff and brought him to the *Arethusa,* where he handed over the basket, which was filled with loaves of bread; then he asked Clarke, with a wink, to count the loaves and see that all was in order. Concealed beneath the loaves were the manuscripts he had paid for, so he gave the porter a handsome tip and sailed away in triumph. So ends Clarke's story of his visit to Patmos.

I READ EXTRACTS from Clarke's account shortly after my first trip here—they were included as part of the potted history in the island's guidebooks. At the time, he struck me as a highly principled, if rather stuffy and xenophobic Englishman who had

done his duty in rescuing rare manuscripts for the world's scholars from what he saw as the ignorant and destructive hands of
the Greeks. He was on a par with his contemporary, the equally
highly principled Thomas Bruce, seventh earl of Elgin, who,
during his service to the nation as envoy extraordinary at the
Sublime Porte, the Ottoman court at Constantinople (1799 to
1802), had formed the purpose of removing from Athens the
celebrated sculptures that came to be known as the Elgin Marbles.
Elgin's self-justification appeared as a pamphlet entitled *Memo-
randum on the Subject of the Earl of Elgin's Pursuits in Greece,*
published in 1810. Clarke's rather lengthier apologia came out
two years later and had run to four editions by 1818.

    Clarke's attitude of contempt toward the Greeks puzzled
me for a time. As a classical scholar with a rooted sympathy
for the place and its culture, it seemed odd that he should hold
in such contempt the descendants of a race for which his background and education must have bred admiration. I did a spot
of research into other British visitors to Greece and discovered
the dismay of classical scholars when their waiters, hoteliers
or guides, although sporting names such as Adonis, Hercules
or even Pericles, turned out to be physically at some remove
from classical nude sculptures and seemed to have little interest in philosophy or art. The German scholar Jakob Fall-
merayer had been able to account for this disparity between
the Greek ideal of the golden age of Pericles and the appearance and behavior of modern Greeks by asserting, in 1835, that
there was no line of descent between the classical and modern
cultures. Modern Greeks, he claimed, were all descendants of
the short brown Slavs who had overrun inhabitants of main-

land Greece in the fifth century. So the modern Greeks could safely be despised.

The word "Greek" in the English and French languages has been colored by contempt: one definition in the *Oxford English Dictionary* is "a cunning, wily person; a cheat," from the early sixteenth century, and a reference is given to the French *un grec*. When I checked this, I found the French had a phrase for cheating at cards: *jouer comme un Grec*. There is also in French the phrase *être Grec,* which means to be too clever or cunning. When Clarke employed Riley to negotiate his purchases as "a person habituated in dealing with knavish Greeks," the phrase "knavish Greeks" was tautological to himself and, he must have assumed, his readers. Byron, after all, had been in his first year at Harrow when Clarke was in Patmos, and Clarke's *Travels* was published in 1812—the same year that *Childe Harold* appeared and Byron awoke and found himself famous. Hellenophilia was not yet quite in fashion.

The London Library, with its customary awesome efficiency and courtesy, sent the Clarke volumes to me on Patmos. I remember that on first reading them it struck me as odd that he should describe the cave of St. John as not spacious enough for a hermit, when we often saw up to fifty people in the tiny church which now occupies it. I was telling Felicia the full story one day when she said: "But I don't believe him. How could the abbot have been illiterate when there was the Patmian School?" I decided to go up to the monastery and investigate.

The librarian, Chrysostomos, had become a friend and I asked him if he would help me to check up on some of Clarke's less likely statements. I first needed to find out whether the monk who was abbot in October 1801 was indeed illiterate. This was not difficult. The library holds a list of the names of past abbots, from which we were able to see that the monk who held office from July 1801 to sometime in 1804 was Parthenios Negropontis, also known as Bronzis. He had traveled widely as a young man, collecting tribute from the monastery's properties in Asia Minor, and he signed his name with a practiced flourish. He also had a small private library, which he donated to the monastery.

As to the reference to the "ignorant monks" and the statement that "neither the Superior nor his colleagues were able to read," Chrysostomos confirmed that apart from the odd hermit or country dweller, the monks were all educated at the Patmian School. The level of their education is shown in the story of the arrival of the French traveler Choisseul-Gouffier in 1780. As his ship pulled into the harbor, a breathless monk, who had run down the mountain at the sight of the French flag, shouted to him, in French, to ask urgently whether Voltaire was still alive.

The Patmian School, where, according to Clarke, "Greek families send their sons to be educated by a set of monks unable to read their own or any other language," was founded in 1713 by Makarios Kaloyeras, a Patmian by birth who was educated in Constantinople. A student of his, the Russian Barskij, wrote:

> He transformed many fishermen and peasants into
> philosophers and theologians . . . one finds them not only
> here but scattered in other neighbouring lands and so the
> teaching of Greek grammar and philosophy has been

enriched since 1720 . . . The island of Patmos had been deserted and unknown, but now it is famous everywhere because, for the enslaved Greeks under the Muslim yoke, this school has taken the place of ancient Athens.

At the time of Clarke's visit the Patmian School was under the supervision of one Daniel Kerameus, who, far from being unable to write, was the author of five books on Greek grammar, one of which is still in the monastery library, dated 1785. Many of his pupils became eminent in church and state.

Clarke states clearly that he found the Plato among the heap of documents rotting on the library floor, a prey to damp and rats. The abbot referred to them merely as "manuscripts" while "turning up his nose with an expression of indifference and contempt." Was he not, then, aware of the value that had been set on them by past visitors or by past catalogues?

From its beginnings, the Monastery of St. John on Patmos had been a scholarly institution. The founder, St. Christodoulos, had donated his books to form the nucleus of a library and given instructions for its enlargement through purchases, donations and copying. All the monks were from the beginning trained in calligraphy and had a duty to report to the abbot on their work as copyists. The first catalogue of the library dates from 1103, and by 1200 a further catalogue lists 268 codes on parchment, as well as texts of the liturgy, biographies of saints and even one classical text, the *Categoriae* of Aristotle.

A marginal note illustrates that the monks and copyists had a keen sense of the value of the manuscripts by at least one of them, written in 1180:

> I, Neilos, great sinner and unlettered peasant do this little book, penned by me, dedicate to the greatly venerated and holy Convent of Patmos, that the saint might be mindful of me: not because the Convent lacketh books—perish the thought for what Monastery worthy of respect has as many scribes and calligraphists as this one . . . Whosoever would deprive this hilly Monastery of this, Neilos's gift, on any pretext, be it just or no, let him be accursed and damned. So be it! Amen.

The dedicator of a later codex, dated 1494, is even more emphatic in his condemnation of anybody who should dare to remove it, even for the worthiest educational purpose:

> . . . and if anyone giveth this book to the pupils while at lessons, thus causing its destruction, may the curses of the 300 saintly and godly fathers at the Synod of Nicaea and the leprosy of Gehazi fall upon him and may he have the great St. John and the Blessed Father Christodoulos as his accusers on the Day of Judgement.

Can we believe that the abbot turned up his nose at manuscripts that had been venerated within his monastery for centuries? The catalogues had been regularly updated, and by 1785, sixteen years before Clarke's arrival, a French visitor declared it to be the best organized that he had seen.

What seemed to be emerging from the growing evidence was that Clarke's account of his visit was not simply flawed by honest mistakes such as any traveler on a brief visit to the island might have made. At the time of writing his book he was concious that his removal of the manuscripts was no longer generally accepted by the British public as a right to which their nationality entitled them. The Elgin Marbles had aroused controversy, and so Clarke had to justify his taking the manuscripts from Patmos by claiming he acted in the interests of preservation and international scholarship. He chose to do so by stressing that the monks in whose care he found them were ignorant and illiterate and had no idea of their value—an invention of his own prejudice—and that the situation in which he found the manuscripts was one of total neglect, which in the light of evidence from other visitors to the library seems to be plainly untrue.

I was becoming very interested in Clarke himself. He was emerging as a free spirit with a lively imagination untrammeled by the caution and scruples associated with classical scholarship. I looked him up in the eleventh edition of the *Encyclopaedia Britannica,* which is, in Patmos, my main source of contact with the outside world. He was not, it turns out, a classical scholar. He is described as a "mineralogist and traveller," who spent his early years as a traveling companion to young men of means and built up a reputation for shipping home valuable antiquities. His doctorate was granted to him by the University of Cambridge, not for scholarship but as a result of the valuable donation he had made to the university of a colossal statue of the Eleusinian Ceres. He sold manuscripts (including the Plato from Patmos) to the Bodlean Library for £1,000, and the *Britannica* goes on to record that out of the publication of his travels he made a clear profit of £6,595.

Clarke was clearly not an idealistic intellectual but an entrepreneur with an eye to the main chance. This is confirmed by a biography published after his death by an admiring contemporary, the Reverend W. Otter, who charts his hero's progress with an excess of charity. He begins in grammar school, where the headmaster reported Clarke deficient in application and finally "notorious with his schoolfellows not only for the neglect of his own exercises but for the ingenious and good-natured tricks which he played to interrupt the labours of others." He entered Cambridge University at the age of sixteen years, which might seem strange, writes his biographer, there being "clearly no reason arising from his proficiency which called for early admission into academic life"; but a friend of his father's had been master of Jesus College and managed to arrange that he be sent there as a chapel clerk.

At Cambridge, where the Reverend Otter was his contemporary, Clarke behaved as he had at grammar school, showing no interest in his studies but only "the same playful and welcome interruption of the more measured and regular labours of others." In his final year, when most students were bent over their books, Clarke "busied himself constructing a large balloon, which he released from the grass-plat within the cloisters of the college to the applause of a great concourse of people."

But he was again lucky in his choice of friends. Having passed through Cambridge University, in the words of his admiring biographer, "not only without academical honours or distinctions of any kind but . . . without even those moderate advantages which a common mind might have derived from it," he was placed in the final examinations "with the seasonable assistance" of a fellow of the college.

Clarke describes in a letter how he acquired the Eleusinian Ceres, which earned him his doctorate in spite of the opposition of the Eleusinian peasants, who feared that their crops would fail if he took her away. "I went to Athens and made application to the Pacha, aiding my request by letting an English telescope glide between his fingers. The business was done; the telescope and the popularity of the English name at present in Turkey determined the affair."

On Patmos he did not even need a telescope. We shall never know exactly what arrangements he made, but the story of his visit has gone down in the oral history of the monks here, with an astonishing sequel. In the version told to me by the librarian, the monks start by saying that Clarke was allowed to see the books only because he threatened them with a letter from the Turkish governor, of whom they were afraid. They say that, far from being indifferent to the collections in the library, when the loss of the books was discovered the monks were scandalized and demanded to know who was responsible. Nobody would confess, and yet it was clear that Clarke must have had an accomplice. The abbot agreed to organize a formal ceremony to express the shock and horror the monks felt by excommunicating the guilty party.

The *aphorismos,* or excommunication, was witnessed by the people of Chora. Then, monks assembled in Agia Levia Square, in the center of town, dressed in black and carrying lighted black candles. The abbot, Parthenios Negropontis (Bronzis), pronounced the solemn words of excommunication of the unknown monk responsible for the great loss the monastery had suffered. As he did so, out of a calm clear day came a sudden powerful gust of wind that tore from his head the *epanokalimavko*—the embroidered cloth that is the symbol of his authority—and carried it away. It was never found. The other monks' headdresses were undisturbed.

Among the words of the *aphorismos* is a declaration that the guilty person's body will not decompose after death. Bronzis died of an apoplexy in 1812. The bones of the monks are kept in an ossuary which is an outbuilding of the Church Panagia Kimitirion, the parish church close to Agia Levia Square. According to Papa Giorgi, the jovial parish priest, there is a body among them which has not yet completely decayed. It is that of Bronzis.

It is quite possible that Clarke never went to the library of the monastery. He describes it as a small oblong chamber with a vaulted stone roof. At the time of his visit, the library, which had a flat beamed wooden ceiling, was being enlarged, and it is likely that the books and manuscripts, which had long been the treasures of Patmos, were in a temporary storeroom. If the manuscripts were indeed on the floor, it is possible they were stacked there awaiting transportation to the new library, which was opened the year after his visit. Some indication of the monks' attitude toward the possessions which Clarke wrote were of no consequence to them may be gathered from the plaque they cut in marble and set over the entrance to the library after he left:

PSYCHIS IATREION

ATTENTION! HERE ARE MANY FAMOUS
MANUSCRIPTS AND BOOKS, TO A WISE MAN
MORE ENDURING THAN GOLD. TAKE CARE
TO GUARD THEM BETTER THAN YOUR
LIVES. IT IS BECAUSE OF THEM THAT THIS
BUILDING IS A BEACON OF LIGHT. 1802

The heading of the notice gives a name to the library to which
any lover of books will respond. *Psychis* means "of the soul" and
iatreion is a place where doctors work: a surgery or clinic.

So we may translate it as "A Place of Healing for the Soul."

Ten

ᐰ TAKING THE PLUNGE

PATMOS HAD MADE adjustments to our attitudes toward history, diet, punctuality and the need for a sense of urgency in life. It was time for me to look again at religion.

Those people who are paid to tell us why we behave as we do often say that our religious orientation depends on the society we live in. There is, as one sociologist wrote, a "vexed connection between what we believe and who we sup with." We get our notions about the world from other human beings, it is said, and these notions continue to be plausible to us because others continue to affirm them. And that seems to me to be true—up to a point. I spent most of my time for fifteen years among Fijians without being drawn to the view that human affairs are watched over by Dakuwaqa, the shark god.

Of course, it will be objected that I am not a Fijian, that our cultures are too remote to influence each other; but then neither am I a Greek. Many aspects of the Greek view of the world seem to me alien: the notion, for example, that the most desirable human situation is to be with a lot of people making a lot of noise at around 2 A.M.; or the way in which information in Greece as to future events, such as weather forecasting or ferry arrival times, is based not on what is likely but on what would be nice.

But living on Patmos as an agnostic puts you in the situation of being part of what sociologists call a "cognitive minority." A cognitive minority is a group of people whose view of the world differs significantly from the one taken for granted in their society. Christians have been a cognitive minority in Europe for most of the past century, and they have dwindled in numbers during my lifetime to the point at which their sanity may be called into question. After all, the insane are people whose view of the world differs significantly from the one most people take for granted.

I was constantly surprised, on Patmos, by the supernatural element in people's lives: when we thanked our neighbor for a gift of fresh eggs, she would always shake her head, rejecting our gratitude, and say, with a nod of her head to the skies: "*Tou Christou*" ("*From Christ*"). Whenever I picked people up on the road to give them a lift into town they would, as we drove off, cross themselves—which I used to think was a reflection on my driving. And in the evenings the smell of incense would drift down the narrow streets as people censed their icons in a daily ritual. Each autumn, as we said good-bye to friends and added the usual, "See you next spring," they would nod and reply, *"An theli o Theos"* ("God willing").

Most important, I first became aware on Patmos of the operations of what Christians call the Holy Spirit. There is a fascinating theological debate into which I am not qualified to enter as to whether the Holy Spirit is a bird or a gas. What I mean by the phrase is simply a seemingly unaccountable prompting to goodness. We come across this occasionally in Western society and tend to meet it with suspicion. If somebody does me a good turn there has to be a reason; and if we can't see the reason we suspect a hidden agenda. Motiveless benevolence is psychologically inexplicable and defies the law of evolution by natural selection. Nice guys in our world finish last.

But on Patmos I met people whose entire lives seemed influenced by such benevolence. And I realized that the Problem of Goodness is far harder for the agnostic to handle than the more publicized Problem of Evil is for the believer. Motiveless malice is familiar to anybody who keeps up with current affairs; motiveless kindliness is rarer, but more of a mystery.

THE EXPERIENCE OF what seemed to me to be sheer unadulterated goodness in people led me to look again at the Orthodox Christianity that dominates Patmians' lives. Put simply, it had the strongest claim I'd seen to being the closest to the original. I was attracted by the wisdom of the hermits, the spiritual fathers and the monks, nuns and laypeople of Patmos. Of course, there

were the oddities: self-righteous religious individuals and fanatical laypeople. Orthodoxy seems to attract the extremists. But I was
beginning to recognize a flavor of Orthodoxy, which seemed to
me to be consistent, idiosyncratic, lasting and enriching. I wanted
to understand it.

One morning I saw a truck loaded with vegetables for sale
climbing the mountain road up to Chora and heard the voice
of the driver through a battered old metal loudspeaker on the
cab roof. He was shouting: *"Elate na Theete"*—"Come and see."
And the words rang a bell in my mind. They were the same
words Jesus said to the two disciples of John when they were
curious about him; and again in the same first chapter of St. John,
when Nathaniel jokingly asks Philip whether anything good can
come out of Nazareth, the reply is the same: "Come and see."

The vegetable seller was not using a hard-sell technique.
He did not go on about the excellence of his cabbages and potatoes. He said simply, "Come and see—for yourselves. Use your
eyes. Make up your own minds what to buy." Perhaps, I thought,
the time had come for me to do the same: to stop reading about
Christianity and cross-examining Christians; to go into the
Church and see from the inside what was on offer.

There was a problem. I had always assumed that church
is for believers. Churchgoers at every liturgy declare the articles
of their faith in a creed and state publicly that they believe them
to be true. I did not. Belief is the acceptance of a statement as
true. I could not accept as true anything in the creed because the
supporting evidence did not convince me.

This was not for want of research. I had read thousands
of religious books in pursuit of a lifelong interest, interviewed

scores of religious leaders in my work for BBC television and spent hundreds of hours in church. I should have liked Christianity to be true, not least because Felicia was a practicing Christian and it seemed alienating that I could not share her commitment when we were so close in every other way. But she was careful not to put pressure on me and I was scrupulous about not allowing my love for her to sway my commitment to truth.

Then I remembered the story of the Oxford don welcoming his new group of students. He congratulated them on being accepted by the best university in the world and went on to tell them that if they applied themselves with diligence to their studies, they would, three years later, leave Oxford with degrees. "And, gentlemen, you will then," he went on, "know when a man is talking rot. That is to many people the *main,* and to me the *sole,* purpose of an education." I had my degree and had certainly used what education I had to challenge what seemed to me to be false views of reality. And that, of course, is what the intellect does best: it can detect unsound arguments. It is a discriminating function. But it is not sensitive to truths that lie beyond reason, that cannot be explained or expressed rationally. That such truths exist I knew from my experience of great music and from my love for Felicia. Reason had nothing to do with these truths, which I experienced directly and with a certainty that went beyond rational argument.

Faith, I knew, was the acceptance of religious truth through grace. And although grace was possible, although like the Holy Spirit it floated around most places most of the time, none of it had come my way. Or if it had I had not noticed. Perhaps if I could join the Orthodox Church and take part in its liturgy from within, I would be more open to it. But there was a neat circular problem: to join the Church and obtain the grace, I had to recite the creed; I could not recite the creed unless I believed it to be true; and I could not believe it to be true without the grace.

I put the problem to Bishop Kallistos by letter and he replied by return. He knew my situation well and thought I had spent enough time studying Orthodoxy from the outside. My *kairos,* as he put it, had come. The Greek word means an appropriate time in one's life to do something. It is the word used for "time" in Ecclesiastes: "a time to be born and a time to die; a time to plant and a time to pluck up that which is planted." The time for me to enter the Orthodox Church had come, he thought, and he would be prepared to baptize me on his next visit to Patmos. As for my problem with the creed, the solution was simple: if I could not recite it for myself then he, if I would trust him, would do it for me.

I was shocked at the suggestion. I had always seen baptism as a ceremony in which a converted person filled with shining new certainties was welcomed into the Church. The recital of the creed was a public declaration by the convert that he had become convinced of these certainties: that God exists, that Jesus Christ was his only son, that he was born of a virgin, that he rose from the dead. I could not honestly say I accepted any of these propositions. So how could I present myself for baptism?

Yet I had developed a liking, which had grown into an affinity and eventually an admiration, for people who did seem to accept these unlikely notions. How was this possible? If a man tells you there are fairies at the bottom of his garden you do not give much weight to the rest of his opinions; you might even shy

away from his company. But I was happy with people who re-
cited every Sunday a creed which I could not accept. Was I becoming a Christian by proxy?

I had to accept that Bishop Kallistos was a man of wide
experience and great learning. More important, he knew me
well, I had kept constantly in touch with him and he probably
was more aware of my spiritual condition than I was. Felicia
had often told me that the nuns of Evangelismos would say to
her, "Don't worry about Peter. He is already Orthodox. It's just
that he is the only one who doesn't know it." And then I remembered the words of Robert Runcie, archbishop of Canter-
bury, that "Christianity is an experiment which leads to an
experience which is verifiable as you go along." I decided to
start the experiment.

I have described the ceremonies of initiation. Although the
photographs record that I emerged from the experience flushed
and excited, I did not see any blinding lights during or after my
total immersion. No certainties were revealed. I emerged still
agnostic, but with a difference. A part of me was opened that
had been shut. I heard no messages, but felt ready to receive
them. If I had received grace, it had come in the form of an increase not in conviction, but in awareness, in receptivity.

Very soon, after my second or third communion, I realized
that I was beginning to experience as realities what I had taken
to be colorful imagery. The divine energies present in the mystery of the Eucharist open within us a capacity to see, or to sense,
spiritual realities to which we were insensible. That sentence is
a myth for those without the experience; a reality for those who
have it.

I realized that during the long years I had spent studying Christianity to see whether or not I found it credible, I was missing the point. The creeds of the Church do not contain the Christian truth that Christ said would set us free. They were formalized and written down in response to challenges from outside, when the Church was forced to defend itself by using the language of philosophy to define its dogma. But that language belonged to the world of concepts against which the Church was attempting to defend itself. Most important, the Greek philosophers were building systems of thought by using terms that became part of the vocabulary of individuals whether or not they were able to experience the realities those terms expressed.

The full doctrine of the Church was made available only to baptized Christians. It still is. Much of it is written and so accessible to all, but the most important aspects are passed on orally and symbolically because they can only be transmitted to someone who is ready to receive them. And by their very nature they cannot be written. By taking the first step, by being baptized into the Orthodox Church, I had not experienced any new convictions but had opened myself to an evolving mystery which the Church has preserved and which exists to communicate to its members.

And, on Patmos, I had become normal.

Eleven

☞ DIFFERENCES

THE QUESTION MOST frequently asked of the Orthodox by Western Christians is: What are the differences between East and West and do they matter? The answer is that there are differences of practice and of belief. They do matter, though not all of them equally. Whole libraries of books have been written on these questions, and I shall attempt a summary here. If you are not interested, please skip to the next chapter.

The occasion of the Great Schism between the Orthodox East and the Latin West was a colorful and theatrical event. On Saturday, July 16, 1054, the clergy and people were assembling for the liturgy in Agia Sophia, the Orthodox cathedral of Constantinople. A solemn procession of three entered the building: two cardinals and an archbishop. They were legates of the pope of Rome. They marched into the sanctuary and placed on the altar a Bull of Excommunication containing an anathema of the patriarch and his followers. As they left, their leader, Cardinal Humbert, paused at the western door to shake the dust ceremonially from his feet. Jesus had instructed his disciples to do this when leaving the house of the unworthy.

THE POMP AND CIRCUMSTANCE OF THIS STORY have ensured its place in histories of Christianity, though it does have its problems. I always wonder, for example, how a cardinal in full regalia can shake the dust from his feet without looking faintly ridiculous. And historians, who are allergic to simple explanations and love to muddy the waters, have been quick to point out that the real situation is more complicated. The cardinal and his colleagues, as it happened, had no authority on that famous day because the Pope Leo IX, whose personal legates they were, had died three months before. So the excommunication was invalid. Further, nobody at the time seemed to notice or to mind very much. Although the patriarch, Michael Celarius, excommunicated those who had excommunicated him, contemporary writers virtually ignore what happened. The *communio in sacris* of pilgrims coming from the West to Jerusalem via Constantinople continued and the Latin Rite churches, which the patriarch closed down, were soon open again.

At the heart of the Great Schism was the question of the position of the pope. The Western Church taught that he was the vicar of Christ on earth and the supreme authority to whom all human beings must submit if they wish to be saved. This teaching is, characteristically, supported by what appears to be a watertight rational argument.

It is only reasonable to assume, runs the apologia, that if Christ founded a church he would have taken steps to ensure that it would endure and be properly organized. Any organization needs a head. Christ appointed one in the clearest possible terms, saying to the apostle Peter, "Thou art Peter and upon this rock will I build my church and the gates of hell shall not prevail against it. And I will give to thee the keys of the kingdom of heaven; and whatsoever thou shalt bind on earth it shall be bound also in heaven; and whatsoever thou shalt loose on earth it shall be loosed also in heaven" (Matthew 16:17–19). The clear and obvious meaning of these words is that Peter was appointed supreme head of the Church, that he was given the power of legislative and judicial authority over it and that the test of membership in the Church was the capacity to recognize him in that office. The history of the Church seems to support this.

After the death and resurrection of Jesus, Peter went to Rome and became its bishop. His first epistle is dated from that city, and it was in Rome that he was martyred. The list of his successors in that see are recorded, from Linus, Anacletus and Clement down to the pope of today, in an unbroken succession of pastors who have been recognized throughout the Church as the vicars of Christ on earth, to whom the keys of the kingdom have been passed by succession and who have indeed taken the crossed keys as the symbol of their authority. The words of Christ to Peter are emblazoned in Latin around the dome of

St. Peter's Church, the mother church of the entire Christian world.

From the Eastern perspective, it seems odd that St. Mark, known as St. Peter's interpreter and companion, and who was with him in Rome, should not have noticed these crucial words of Christ to his master. They are found only in Matthew. And there the power of binding and loosing is given not to Peter alone, but to all the disciples. Although the inscription in Latin around the dome of St. Peter's is redolent of high antiquity, the original words, of which the Latin is a mistranslation, were written in Greek.

The tense of the Greek verb makes it clear that Peter's actions in binding and loosing shall be in line with what has been bound and loosed in heaven. In other words, his decisions will be in accordance with the divine will, rather than heaven waiting for him to speak before making up its mind. It is, of course, impossible for us to know with certainty what the *ipsissima verba,* the true words of Christ, were; but even if He did suggest that the position of Peter in the Church which he would found was authoritative, there is no indication that his authority would pass to successors or how those successors would be chosen.

In the years leading up to the Schism, it would have been hard for the Eastern patriarchs to have taken seriously the claim that the popes of Rome were the vicars of Christ on earth and had inherited his sanctity and authority. The papacy had been in the gift of the German emperor since King Otto I had had himself crowned emperor by the pope on February 2, 962. He then decreed that all future popes should take the oath of allegiance to his office. In the following century, twenty-one out of twenty-five popes were handpicked by the German crown.

They did not do a good job. Simony flourished; popes had their mistresses; and they were poisoned, strangled or just mutilated by their rivals. By 1045, only nine years before the Great Schism, there was no pope. Instead, there were three rival claimants to the papacy, each with his own army. Then Henry III marched into Italy and got rid of all three, putting a German bishop on the papal throne as Clement II. Clement's first act was to crown the emperor, who then marched back north, leaving Clement with a bodyguard of tall blond Germans. But they were useless against the intrigues of Benedict, one of the three deposed popes, and Clement II soon died from a fatal and obscure poison. Benedict took over, but was deposed again when Henry marched back with Poppo, bishop of Brixen, whom he appointed Pope Damasus II. Although German swords were waved at every passing shadow near the papal residence and the papal kitchens were scrutinized against poison, within three weeks Damasus II was dead, officially of malaria. The emperor, still determined that only a German could be pontiff, appointed Bruno, the bishop of Toul, who had commanded his cavalry, to be Leo IX. It was he who sent Cardinal Humbert to Constantinople.

THE CRUSADES, which proclaimed themselves as a pious campaign to free the sacred places of Christendom from the hands of the Turks, completed the breach between East and West. After the First Crusade, the crusaders set up Latin patriarchs at Antioch

and Jerusalem, resulting in local schisms between the Greeks and
Latins. Then, in 1204, the notorious Fourth Crusade sacked Constantinople with such eye-catching savagery that even the Arab
historians record it as one of the most reprehensible acts in history.
Thousands were slaughtered in the streets. Priests and monks
came out of Agia Sophia carrying crosses and Bibles and begging
for their lives. They were massacred by the Frankish mercenar-
ies, who then plundered the church and, it is recorded, set a pros-
titute on the patriarch's throne to sing lewd songs while drunken
soldiers raped Greek nuns in the neighboring monasteries.

From this time forth the Christian East and the Christian
West were separate and alienated, each claiming to be the true
Church. The origins of their differences went back to apostolic
times. Christianity originally spread in a Mediterranean world
that was unified by the Roman Empire. But from the third century, that empire was divided into two parts, eastern and western, each with its own emperor. The barbarian invasions of the
fifth century destroyed the Western Empire, and although
Byzantium continued to think of Rome as part of the universal
Christendom, the political unity had been destroyed. When
Pope Stephen became the first bishop of Rome to cross the Alps
in November 753, he was turning his back on Constantinople.
His journey was to seek from the West the help he had been
denied in the East. Under threat from the Lombards, he needed
the troops of Pepin, king of the Franks. That journey changed
the orientation of the papacy toward the West. The creation
of the Holy Roman Empire fifty years later completed the alien-
ation of Rome from Byzantium. This too had its culminating
theatrical moment of symbolism on Christmas Day, 800. At

St. Peter's tomb, Pope Leo III placed an imperial crown on the head of Charlemagne, joined the congregation in proclaiming him "Caesar" and "Augustus" and then knelt in homage before him.

More important for Christianity than the political estrangement between Constantinople and Rome were the different attitudes that had developed in East and West toward the organization of the Christian Church and the doctrines it taught. These differences continue. To deal first with the organization: that of the Eastern Church has always been collegial; that of the West developed into a monarchy.

The East was the birthplace of Christianity; it has many churches that were founded in apostolic times. The bishops who teach its doctrines are all equal in authority. All have a duty to maintain the tradition. Indeed, the East goes so far as to claim that the bishops derive their authority from the tradition and not the other way about. The decisions of the bishops made in ecumenical councils are binding on the faithful because they maintain the tradition, and not because the bishops made them.

The West has only one great see that claims apostolic foundation—Rome. So Rome became vested, in the West, with a unique power, and its bishop claimed absolute authority over his Church. The East was content so long as he exercised that authority only within the Western Church. In fact, the East had always recognized the pope as the first bishop in the Church. But the pope, according to Orthodoxy, is the first bishop among equals. When he tries to exercise an immediate power of jurisdiction over the universal Church, he is going beyond his authority; when he claims infallibility as his own prerogative he is wrong.

It is true that the East encouraged this assertion of papal supremacy by not protesting against it. Orthodox writers have suggested that this was because the concept of collegiality was so strong in the East that the churches there could not take seriously the papal claims. They could not believe that the pope, as a Christian bishop, could possibly claim for himself sovereign jurisdiction over the whole Church. Even when the legate of Pope Celestine declared at the Council of Ephesus in 431 that "Peter, to whom our Lord Jesus Christ has given the keys of the Kingdom and the power to bind and loose sins, now and for ever more remains and judges in the person of his successors," the Greek bishops said nothing. They remained silent when faced by the triumphalist assertions of Pope Leo the Great, and it is hardly surprising that Rome came to believe that the Eastern churches shared its own conception of papal supremacy.

The Orthodox position has always been that all bishops share equally in the apostolic succession; all have the same sacramental powers; all are divinely appointed teachers of the faith. The pope has a special position of honor as bishop of the city where St. Peter was bishop, and the Orthodox acknowledge Peter as first among the apostles, remembering the "Petrine texts" in the Gospels. Rome was also famous in the earliest times for the firmness with which it opposed heresy, and this is why disputants often turned to Rome for a ruling in matters of doctrine. But the Orthodox reject as untraditional the assertion of the papal bull *Unam Sanctam* of 1302: "We declare, announce and define that it is altogether necessary to salvation for every human creature to be subject to the Roman pontiff."

Orthodox priests may be married or celibate and have to make up their minds which they want to be before they are ordained. This must be a hard choice for a young man who is about to complete his final examinations: he must either find a wife quickly or live celibate for the rest of his life, for he is not allowed to marry after being ordained. Parish priests tend to be married, but their ecclesiastical career prospects are limited: bishops are always elected from the celibate clergy, though an exception is occasionally made for a widower. On Patmos and elsewhere it is becoming increasingly common to appoint a priest-monk in charge of a parish.

It seems to me, from our Patmos experience, that the important difference between our priests and those in the West is one of rank and social position. Training for the priesthood in the West involves a college or university education, and so the priest has a high position in his community. In medieval times he was the only one who could write; today he is a member of an educated elite. On Patmos he is usually a local boy who has attended the same theological college as the rest but who has then been trained at the monastery in liturgical practices. Once ordained, he is necessary to the mystery of the liturgy; he is respected for that, and even elderly relatives will kiss, or try to kiss, his hand. But the kingdom he represents is not of this world. As a young man he is called "Father," but he is not relied on for paternal advice in secular matters. And his status as a priest does not qualify him to hear confessions.

Turning to doctrine, the Christianity proclaimed by Eastern and Western churches is one and the same; but there are important differences of emphasis. The Western Church, influenced by the legalism of Roman culture, has attempted to define and codify the whole of Christianity, from the nature of God to the most refined distinctions concerning the gravity of human sin. The magisterium, or teaching authority of the Roman Church, has erected an immense edifice of dogma, which it describes as a hierarchy of truths, to be accepted by its members. It has also laid down, in its moral theology, the rules and principles according to which human acts must be performed in order for one to attain salvation. So to look briefly at one's own sexual organs in a spirit of curiosity or levity is a venial sin; in mixed bathing, to gaze at the thinly veiled sexual organs of a person of the opposite sex is normally a grave sin, unless the look is brief or from a distance. The Church also teaches that eating two ounces of meat constitutes a grave violation of the law of abstinence, although in the matter of meat soup, four ounces is the equivalent.

The East is less certain, perhaps more confused, about such matters. Not only is the Prodigal Son far and away the most popular story in the Bible, but the Orthodox Church applies what the legal mind would see as a scandalously partial principle of "economy" to its sinners. The aim of economy is the salvation of the soul. The Church has rules but, unlike those of old Israel, they do not strictly bind her. It lies within her power to contravene the strict letter of the law if the purpose of the law will thereby be more fully achieved. Economy, in the eyes of the Orthodox, is closely linked to Philanthropia—loving kindness: the Church, following the example of Christ, makes allowance for men's weakness and never lays a burden on them too heavy for them to bear. Because economy is practical, it changes with circumstances; it does not set a binding precedent.

As for dogma, the Orthodox Church accepts that the essential Christian truth is a mystery. But the word is used in a special sense. It does not mean something totally baffling, as it does when we say, "The workings of a video recorder are a complete mystery to me." In the original Greek, the word *mustirion* is a secret doctrine that is revealed to the *mustis*—the initiated. So the mystery of Christianity is not something that is kept hidden but something that is revealed.

The most important aspect of this is that Christian truth is not an objective series of propositions that can be understood by anybody. It is accessible only to those who have undergone a *metanoia*—a complete change of perspective. This is an attitude to faith well understood in the East, where a religious perspective on life is known to involve the whole person. In the West we recognize as Christian somebody who gives intellectual assent to the propositions in the creed and tries to live a good life. An important consequence of this is that Christianity, for the Orthodox, is a religion of initiates: its most important truths are not contained in its written doctrines but are made available, within the Church, through symbolic transmission, to those who are ready to receive them.

So that the East, possibly as a consequence of its long period of servitude to Islam or Soviet communism, has preserved the primitive Christians' attitude of being a cognitive minority, the salt of the earth. The West, in contrast, set out to conquer the world for Christ on the assumption that all reasonable people would, if confronted by the Christian message, rejoice and accept. When this failed to happen and secular humanism became the settled creed of Western civilization, liberal Protestants lost confidence in the doctrines and began to water them down in the hope of making them more acceptable. A sort of secularized Christianity was preached, without sin or hell or judgment and in which Jesus Christ was a good teacher, along the line of Socrates and Gandhi, but it failed to catch on. The Catholic Church went the other way and condemned attempts to come to terms with the spirit of the times. Orthodoxy, which has known no Reformation, Counter-Reformation, or modernist liberalism, was spared these processes.

But back to the differences: the Protestant Churches are Bible-based. The essential motto of the Reformation was "*Sola scriptura*"—"Only the Scriptures." The Bible contains all that is necessary for salvation, and conversely, if a doctrine is not found in the Bible, it is "unscriptural" and therefore unchristian. The Protestant Churches draw their authority from the same source. They can teach only what is in the Bible and their authority to teach is based on the Bible.

In contrast, the Roman Catholic and Orthodox Churches teach that both Scripture and tradition are necessary. The Bible alone is insufficient because it has to be interpreted. It cannot be set up over the Church because it has to be interpreted within the Church. Since the Bible is the book of the Church, it is reasonable, when in doubt, to ask the Church what it means. Orthodox and Roman Catholic are united in this attitude.

They differ mainly on the question of papal supremacy, discussed above, and on matters of doctrine such as purgatory and the Immaculate Conception, neither of which the Orthodox accept. The doctrine of purgatory teaches that a purification process for the soul is necessary when insufficient penance was done during a person's lifetime for sins which have been forgiven. The practice of giving donations to the Church in order to shorten the time spent in purgatory was one of the scandals which the Reformation attacked. The Immaculate Conception, only formulated in 1854 and frequently misunderstood, teaches that Mary, Mother of God, was conceived as a human being exempt from original sin. Orthodoxy has made no pronouncement on this. The famous issue of the phrase *filioque,* which has often been said to have divided the Churches, seems less important today. But it is constantly brought up, and so it helps to know the true story.

The original creed as defined by the ecumenical councils of Nicaea and Constantinople contained the words "I believe . . . in the Holy Spirit, the Lord, the Giver of Life, who proceeds from the Father . . ." This original form of words is used in the recital of the creed today in the Orthodox Church. Indeed the Council of Constantinople, which finalized the form of words, specifically forbade any addition or deletion.

But the West inserted an extra phrase—*filioque* ("and from the Son")—so that the creed used in the West now reads "proceeds from the Father and the Son." Nobody is quite sure when this interpolation was first used, though it was heard in the Spanish Church at the end of the sixth century. Rome continued to use the original creed, without the *filioque,* until the start of the eleventh century. It then became a cause of dispute between East and West and contributed to the Great Schism of 1054.

There are Orthodox theologians who oppose the additional words on theological grounds, but there are others who accept them as a theological opinion. All Orthodox, however, are united in rejecting the additional words, because the creed belongs to the whole Church and cannot be altered by one branch of it. The West, by adding to the creed, whether or not the addition can be justified, was striking a blow at the unity of the Church.

On Patmos the differences between the Christian Churches are especially noticed, for a number of reasons. The island has been officially proclaimed "holy," and its inhabitants are perhaps therefore acutely conscious of their religious affiliation; Patmos has the connection with St. John, of which it is constantly made aware by streams of pilgrims; and the place was, from 1920 to 1948, part of the Italian colonial empire and under pressure from Rome. So Protestants are accepted more readily than Roman Catholics, because they have never threatened the Church here and there is perhaps a feeling among the Orthodox that Protestants could well be on their way to Orthodoxy. But in fact, nobody seems quite sure what they believe.

Roman Catholics, however, are different. In a church service it is noticed if visitors cross themselves the Roman Catholic way (head, breast, left shoulder) rather than the Orthodox way (head, breast, right shoulder). Sometimes, among the more bigoted, there may be feelings of animosity, though these would not be expressed. The priest will occasionally be put to the embarrassment of having to refuse communion to Roman Catholics who present themselves, reasonably assuming that, since the mutual anathemas between Rome and Constantinople were simultaneously annulled by ceremonies in 1965, the Churches are now in communion. But the Orthodox view is that until unity in the faith has been achieved, there can be no communion in the sacraments. Communion cannot be used as a means to secure unity but must be a consequence of unity achieved. The differences remain.

In my experience, really committed Protestants tend to think of themselves as "saved" because they have accepted Jesus; Roman Catholics, on the other hand, see themselves as "sinners" in need of weekly absolution. Orthodox just think themselves lucky.

There is, it seems to me, enough of the living truth in each of the three Churches to bring its members to Christ. Just as each has enough of fallen humanity to give the Holy Spirit a hard time.

Twelve

☞ AGIO PNEUMA

THE LITTLE CHURCH of the Holy Spirit—in Greek, *Agio Pneuma*—sits high on the western slope of the south island of Patmos, about half a mile from the center of Chora. When we first discovered it the only way to get there was along a narrow goat track that led nowhere else. Below the church, scrub and rough rocks covered the steep slopes down to the sea, and in the early spring they were a blaze of colors: pink and white rock-roses with the bright yellow centers, deep red poppies, marguerites that grew shoulder-high, wild lavender, gladiolus, orchids, cyclamen. Today the mountain has been tragically changed, as we shall hear, but in the first years of our visits, there were only flowers, rocks, goats and birds.

As one looks to the west from the chapel, the sea stretches out to the long shape of Ikaria on the right, and then there's an open sweep of blue out of which, on a clear day, the islands of the Cyclades come into view: Mykonos, Naxos and Amorgós. The setting sun is a spectacular sight from Agio Pneuma, particularly in the few minutes that it hangs over an open sea and sends a broad shimmering scarlet ribbon across the water from the horizon toward you. I got into the habit of walking along the mountain path each evening to catch the spectacle and to exchange a few words with a small, white-haired man who always sat on a wall outside the chapel to watch. My Greek was very poor and, although I always carried a dictionary, we never had what could be called a real conversation; but he was always glad to see me and patient with my struggles to understand him.

I did manage to find out that he lived close by. His tiny stone hut sat among a cluster of almond trees directly behind the church. There had been some sort of boundary wall around his garden but it had long since broken down and the goats that grazed the mountain wandered freely across what had been cultivated terraces. He told me he had brought up many children there but that they had all gone away and he lived alone. He had neither electricity nor water supplied, but one of his sons had dug a cistern in the garden to catch the winter rains. His home was a single low room built of whitewashed stone with an attached storehouse in concrete blocks. His name was Minas.

It was in the spring of 1990, when a winter of listening to BBC tapes on learning Greek had given me some hope of having a decent conversation with Minas, that I walked out to the church of Agio Pneuma at sunset to find his space on the wall unoccupied. I looked over the broken wall, hoping to see him near the house, and saw that somebody had painted in large blue letters on the whitewashed stone the word "ΠΟΛΙΤΕΙ" ("FOR SALE"). The place was empty; the windows were boarded up. Minas was no longer available for worldly conversations.

But I kept up the habit of walking along the mountain track to see the sunset from Agio Pneuma. Often Felicia would come with me during the spring and summer to watch the red globe as it sank in the open sea, a little farther north each evening until it reached Ikaria and set behind the hills. After June 21, when it set into a particular V shape on the Ikarian profile at 8:34 P.M., it began the return journey across the Cyclades, setting a little farther south a little earlier each evening.

The following year, on our sunset walk, we noticed that the "ΠΟΛΙΤΕΙ" sign was still painted on the wall, though its color was fading. The house was still empty, but there were a few chickens in the garden, sharing a fenced enclosure with half a dozen rabbits. Goats had the run of the garden. The concrete block storehouse had a metal door with an open barred window in it. Jumping through the bars, in and out, was a troop of rats, and when we looked in we saw that a heap of grain had been tipped onto the floor to feed the rabbits and chickens. The rats scuttled past us as we peered in. We left quickly.

A few months later, as we were riding back to Chora on the motorbike after a swim, we stopped to look up at the monastery from the south side. The view is striking and one of the most familiar of the Patmos color postcards. As we looked up at the massive turreted walls of the monastery, towering over the white houses of Chora packed around it, we noticed, perhaps for the first time, way over to the left on the mountain ridge, at quite a distance from Chora, the tiny isolated red roof of Agio Pneuma church. And the mad thought struck us that this would be a wonderful place to live.

The Chora house was comfortable. We had electricity, town water, rubbish collection, friendly neighbors. We had been accepted into the context of life in the town. We could walk to the shops or restaurants in less than five minutes. Yes, life was comfortable. And yet, we were used to living in a silent place. Our house in England was down a half-mile farm track surrounded by fields and forests, with no other house in sight. It seemed ironic that we had come to Patmos to live in society. Wouldn't it be an improvement to move out onto the mountain, to the peace and seclusion of Agio Pneuma?

Marouso, our first friend and neighbor, was horrified at the idea. "You can't live out on the mountain," she said. "It is a wild place. There is no light, no electricity and no water. And it is so far away. I have lived here all my life *and I have never even been there.*" Every word she said made the place seem more tempting, and we decided to start a few inquiries. We knew enough about purchasing property in Greece to realize that the chances were very slim; but Agio Pneuma seemed worth it.

The first problem was to find out who the owners were. This took some time and involved a few false leads. But then I heard that Minas had a widow named Maria and that she lived in a rooming house that was the last building in Chora before the track to Agio Pneuma started. Confident with my BBC Greek, I went to see her one afternoon and told her how much we loved the place, how I had enjoyed my conversations with

Minas and how much we would like to buy the house. Maria was sympathetic. She understood our love for the place and said how delightful it would be if we could become neighbors. But then she shook her head sadly. The house had been sold already, she said, for an enormous sum of money to a rich American. He would soon be rebuilding it. He just had not got around to painting out the sign.

We accepted the news without too much stress. The site was a magnificent one, and no doubt the rich American would build a luxury villa there to visit for a couple of weeks every year; but we were happy enough in our Chora house. Felicia was painting and I could write there during the mornings when the neighbors thought we were back in bed. We could visit Agio Pneuma at sunset and enjoy the spectacle.

So the summer passed and we made our regular trips along the mountain track, expecting every evening to find the little stone hut of Minas—which we called Agio Pneuma, after the church—surrounded by bags of cement and scaffolding. They would have to be carried there by donkeys, and the rich American was going to need lots of time, money and patience to make Agio Pneuma habitable to civilized standards of comfort. It was going to be an interesting diversion on our sunset walks. But 1991 came and went, and nothing happened.

The following spring we noticed that the chickens had increased to around twenty, that there were a few tethered goats in the garden and that the rabbits were in force, but that the rich American had not yet made an impact. We decided he must be a victim of the planning department's commitment to procrastination. What would happen if he ran out of patience—rich

Americans don't like to be pushed around. Perhaps he would give up the whole idea and we would have another chance to buy the place. And yet he must have paid lots of money for it . . .

One evening we were playing around with daydreams when I noticed a stooping figure wearing a black plastic imitation of a Sherlock Holmes deerstalker hat walking through the almond trees. He produced a key and went into the rat-ridden storehouse, coming out again with an enamel dish of grain, which he threw to the chickens. We recognized Alexis, who had married Maria's daughter and lived with her in the rooming house. He was not a great communicator, but we had a brief chat. He told me that the chickens and rabbits were his; that he had moved them there after the death of Minas because he was short of space at home; that he enjoyed the walk out to feed them each day. When I asked for news of the rich American, he had none. But he was quite sure that any day the builders would be arriving.

That evening Felicia and I discussed the situation at Agio Pneuma, and a light slowly dawned: Alexis was enjoying the use of the garden at Agio Pneuma until the rich American arrived. It had been over two years since he'd bought the house, an unusually long time of inactivity, even on Patmos. How lucky for Alexis. How much luckier still he would be if the rich American never appeared again, because then the house could never be sold to anyone else. How even better off he would be if there *were* no rich American. Finally, we reflected, what better way is there to put off prospective buyers of a property you want to make use of than to tell them it has already been sold?

We had broken the first rule of living on Patmos, which is: do not believe everything you are told. Two years late, I began to check up on Maria's story. The first thing I discovered was that she had been living apart from Minas for many years and that the house was owned by one of his sons, Basilis, who had built it. I then found out that Basilis lived in Scala, that he was a sick man, confined to the house, and that he was looked after by a hardworking and intelligent wife called Theologia. I met her and arranged to visit them to talk about buying Agio Pneuma.

It turned out that they were keen to sell the place but had no very lively hopes of doing so. First of all, officially, it was only a house site, since they had not managed to get approval for the buildings they had put up. Secondly, it was so far from Chora that, as Marouso had protested, no local people would move out there. And thirdly, the lack of electricity and water made the conditions far too primitive for anybody but a hermit to be interested in the place. It had been for sale with the sign on display for over two years and not a single person had shown any interest. They were anxious to sell it because their eldest daughter wanted to get married and they were obliged by custom to provide her with a flat.

We arranged to meet at the site the following day so that Felicia could look at the place and decide if we could make it habitable for the two of us with the limited funds we had. When we got there, Theologia opened the low wooden door to the stone house, and we discovered that it was only five meters long and two and a half meters wide. There was a single cot bed, one and a half meters long, on which Minas had slept, and a table and chair which had seen long service. One small window looked to the west and another opened onto the concrete block storehouse, with its heap of corn and scurrying rats. The ceiling had heavy beams of rough-sawn timber which seemed old but solid enough (I tried sticking a penknife blade into them and looking concerned, as I had seen surveyors do back home), with blackened reeds packed above. The floor was compacted earth. There was not a lot to see. No bathroom; not even a lavatory.

But the view was breathtaking: to the south the mountain of Prophet Elias, the familiar jagged triangle with a square white hermitage at the peak; to the west the wide sweep of sea dotted with islands round to Ikaria; to the north and east, fields. The noise level was perfect: there were no sounds at all apart from the wind in the trees. There were the familiar problems of real estate dealings on Patmos: we could not own the property ourselves, nor even have any legal rights to it; any improvements we wanted to make would have to be approved by two authorities, the Byzantine Conservation Department in Rhodes and the planning office on Kalymnos, whose approvals could not be counted on, and whose willingness to even make a decision whilst we were young enough to put it into effect was in question. Agio Pneuma had the additional problem that it did not officially exist. The difficulties being obviously insurmountable, Felicia decided we should go ahead.

This time we did not trouble the notary public. We simply signed a paper in the presence of a friend known both to Theologia and ourselves in which she and Basilis acknowledged receipt of our money and promised that if the authorities ever permitted us to own the house, they would hand it over. At the time, Greece had just become a member of the European Common Market, and there were rumors that the nationals of other Common Market states would be allowed to own property there. There was, in fact, a mechanism in place for appeals against any decision by the authorities refusing non-Greeks permission to own property. But since a decision can only be appealed once it is made, the authorities found a way to retain control: they simply stopped making decisions.

But the important thing was that we were the owners of Agio Pneuma—if not in the eyes of the law, then at least in those of the previous owners. And it was very clear from even the briefest acquaintance with Theologia that she was an honorable person. Our first task was to have the physical existence of our little house acknowledged by law; our second was to get permission to improve it, with funds we hoped to raise by renting out the house in Chora.

The battles over planning were prolonged and tedious to experience and would be wearisome to read about. Let us skip lightly over them, mentioning only that we managed to persuade people with long memories to testify that the house had been in existence beyond the statutory period necessary for it to be registered. The skirmishes over permission for a bathroom and kitchen were conducted with tenacity and skill by our agents, Costas and Matoula, who were quite ready to seize by the arm visiting officials from Rhodes or Kalymnos and propel them to the site. There remained only the little matter of raising cash.

This was settled in the smoky bar of the ferry *Ialysos* as it plowed through the stormy Cyclades toward Piraeus the following October. We fell into conversation with a German doctor and his wife who had been on holiday on Patmos at the invitation of mutual friends. They had very much enjoyed the holiday, and had even thought of buying a house on the island. But all the properties they had been shown were too large and expensive. Money was not the problem. They had houses in other parts of the world and expected to have the time to visit Patmos only for a couple of weeks or so every two years. It did not make sense to buy a large place.

Felicia began to talk about our Chora house, then sketched its layout on the back of a beer mat. The doctor was fascinated—it turned out he had always wanted to be an architect, was fascinated by three-dimensional drawings and had turned his obsession with three-dimensionality to professional use by becoming an orthopedic surgeon. When we said our good nights, he was full of regrets that they had not seen our house, which seemed to be, he said, all they wanted. Sadly, he added, they would not be returning to Patmos for a couple of years.

But a seed had been sown. We happened to meet them next morning, and Felicia said that she had a set of architect's plans of the house back in England. The doctor's eyes lit up, and he said he would love to see them. Things moved quickly. A couple of days later he rang me to say he had received the plans and some photos and had no doubt that he wanted the house. He was happy to pay the price we asked, he said, and if I would settle the final details with his brother, who was a lawyer, we could go ahead.

I knew, of course, that we could go nowhere. Once any lawyer had a sniff of the arrangements, he would cry havoc. No sane adult human being, let alone one professionally committed to skepticism in human affairs, could possibly agree to what we proposed. The telephone conversation that evening was remarkable for the iron control with which a German lawyer suppressed his shrieks of disbelief at the sheer idiocy of my replies:

"I understand you have a property on Patmos which you wish to sell to my brother. You are in possession of the deeds?"

"Well, no, actually. The house is registered at the office of the notary public."

"Then it is registered in your name."

"Well, not exactly."

"Then you are not the legal owners."

"That's right. But the Greek lady who does own it is very nice. She used to be a primary school teacher. She promised to hand over the place if the law ever changes. You see, we're not allowed to own property on Patmos . . ."

"And my brother?

"Well, he can't either. Not yet. You see, it's a frontier territory . . ."

"So you are proposing to sell to my brother unenforceable rights to a house which is not yours, which is registered to somebody else and which cannot be registered to him?"

"That's about the size of it. But one day things may change . . ."

"And if that day never arrives, you will undertake to refund his money?"

"Not really. You see, we need it to spend on another house."

"I think you would agree, it would be unwise for him to proceed?"

"It would be quite insane."

"Thank you. Good-bye."

It was about half an hour later when the phone rang again. It was our German doctor. His brother had called him in an unusually emotional state and protested at the complete inanity of the proposal. So he had decided to go ahead. If we would agree to pass over to him whatever flimsy rights we had to the house, he would send us the money. I remembered our original purchase of the house under the trees by the little chapel with Father Amphilochios. Once again, our Chora house had been bought by someone who had never seen it.

Thirteen

☞ Taking Possession

When you buy a property in most countries you get what is called "vacant possession." This means that when you take over the place you are on your own. With Agio Pneuma, things were different. Of course, we did not own the place—we had paid for it but it still belonged to the original owners. And what we did not get for our money was vacant possession.

First of all there were the goats, five of them: one billy, two nannies and two kids. They had been born and raised on the place and as far as they were concerned, they had priority. As we approached, they would glance up for a moment, a look of mild curiosity flickering across those yellow eyes behind the haughty noses, and then drop their heads again and get on with demolishing whatever foliage was to hand. Then there were the chickens, scratching the earth behind the goats to complete the desertification of what we had hoped might be our garden terraces. The rabbits were behind a fence, but judging by their numbers had clearly been active in their confinement.

Alexis had left his stock in the garden over winter, which was not unreasonable since, although he knew we had bought the place, we were not using it. I decided that as soon as we made a great show of tidying up around the house, he would come along and remove them. The first thing to do was to rescue the concrete block storehouse from the rats, who were very obviously in possession of it. We did this by opening the metal doors and charging in, beating tin cans and screaming as we rushed around the heap of grain on the floor. The rats scuttled out and we shut the doors and the windows that were set in the doors' upper half. Then we tried to scoop up the grain into black plastic dustbin bags; but as soon as we plunged our hands into what we had taken for a heap of inert cereal seed, it began to heave and vibrate. At least 10 percent of the heap was alive. It comprised bugs, beetles, termites, earwigs, cockroaches, millipedes, centipedes, spiders and scorpions. There may well have been an even richer tapestry of wildlife than that, but we did not carry out a close examination.

Fortunately we had brought out from England the sort of stout gardening gauntlets provided as protection against the gentler annoyances of the horticultural scene there, so we donned these and carried on scooping. Most of what went into the plastic bags was grain because anything that could wriggle or scuttle did so as we scooped out the handfuls and the mobile part of

the heap separated itself and rushed out into the garden or cow-
ered in corners, to be flushed out later. After a couple of hours
we had four large black bags of (mainly) grain outside the storehouse and a swept floor within.

The next morning when we arrived, hoping that Alexis
would have realized we were moving in and might have shifted
his animals, they were still in settled possession. The only change
was the frantic activity of the rats, which were scuttling up the
metal doors and hurling themselves against the closed windows
of what had been their storehouse. For a couple of weeks we
visited the site every day to clear away piles of rubbish: old tires,
rusty metal sheeting and wire netting, odd shoes and empty food
cans. We did not see Alexis during this time, and I was trying
to screw up the courage and muster the vocabulary to visit him
at his house when one evening we happened to meet on a street
in Chora and I asked him if he yet knew when he might be able
to move his stock.

Alexis clutched at his chest and reeled back against the wall
of a house. He began to shout a stream of words that I could only
half understand. I was driving him to madness; forcing his family into starvation. Where could he take his goats—goats that
he loved more than he did people? How could I suddenly demand, on five minutes' notice, that he drive them away? And
his poor hens would starve and fall dead from their perches
because of my cruelty.

I kept stammering that there was really no hurry. It had
only been six months since we'd bought the house and of course
he could have all the time he liked to find another place for his
stock. We wanted only to be good neighbors . . . But Alexis was

writhing against the wall in spasms of agony and I was getting scared. He looked as though he might have a heart attack and was shouting so continuously that he could not hear what I was saying. Then a neighbor turned up who caught on to what was happening and managed to calm Alexis down. As he tottered away, the neighbor explained that naturally Alexis had been frustrated when somebody had taken over a property he'd hoped would quietly fall into his hands. There was really no problem. He had other chickens in other places and the goats could graze over the whole mountain. But I would certainly understand why he was upset.

I was shaken at having caused such a violent scene and wondered if we had made a mistake in swapping our peaceful town house with its friendly neighbors for an isolated broken-down shack infested with rats and scorpions where the nearest neighbor was hostile. But the next day the goats were gone, and that evening, after dusk, Alexis arrived to collect the roosting and somnolent hens from their perches in the hut. He was perfectly cheerful and lost his serenity only when, the hens having been safely stowed, one small but alert cockerel danced away from his grasping fingers and kept its liberty. He apologized for this and said he would be back the next morning to take it away.

We felt that he was being simpleminded in hoping to catch a cockerel in the light of day. We had kept hens and knew well the agility and inventiveness of a free-range cock. Ours had had their flight feathers trimmed and could be herded into a corner and picked up; but this one could fly to the top of any tree it liked. Alexis was, we thought, not experienced in the ways of poultry.

We were convinced of this when he arrived with a pullet under his arm. She was young, he explained, and very desirable. He was quite sure the cockerel would come to her.

Then he disappeared into the hen hut. After a short time the pullet came strutting out and began scratching in the dust of the yard. She certainly looked trim and sleek; we were ready to take the word of Alexis that she was desirable. As she ranged about ten yards from the door of the hut, the cockerel flew down from a tree and began to strut around in front of her. She seemed pleased by the attention but responded by backing away from him, an action we had never seen before. Again he strutted and crowed; again she backed away. And then we saw the string attached to her left leg, which was being pulled taut from inside the hut. After about five minutes the pullet was standing on the threshold of the hut, with the cockerel dancing a few feet from her. Then she suddenly disappeared inside, and he followed. There was a scuffle; a cloud of dust came out of the doorway, followed by a triumphant Alexis, with the cockerel in his hands. He knew more about chickens—certainly Patmos chickens, at least—than we did.

It was about six weeks before we were left alone at Agio Pneuma. Every day somebody seemed to turn up to collect something. As we had no boundary wall or gate, they simply walked in and picked up whatever they wanted. We hoped to have a garden made fertile by the goat and hen droppings, and were dismayed when one day a couple of men with sacks came and dug away all the soil and manure left by the goats, hens and rabbits. This seemed an infringement of our rights, but we were not at all sure what our rights were and certainly could not insist on them. We later learned from a goatherd who ran a flock of over a hundred on the mountain that the manure is their most valuable product: the milk goes to the goats' kids, but the manure he sells for a thousand drachmas a bag. Patmos is spectacularly infertile.

When it came to the basic building works—putting in a kitchen and lavatory—we had to turn to the professionals. Here it helps to realize that, on Patmos, if you engage a builder, you are likely to have him for life. This is because he will identify himself as your builder and expect to be given any future work you have, and even more so because the other builders will refuse to work for you once you have taken on, and therefore committed yourself, to one. Builders tend to have carpenters who work with them, and it is a good idea to go along with this, because if you follow the practice in other countries of picking your own builder and carpenter, the work tends to come to a halt when the two need to cooperate. Doors and windows are a particular hazard, and stalemate is common when the builder says he is waiting for the carpenter to fit the frames and the carpenter says he is waiting for the builder to complete the architraves.

We had a wild dream of getting electricity to Agio Pneuma—the charm of candles wears thin after a few months, and refrigerators save shopping trips when you are remote. The electricity company offered to extend the line there so long as we paid for all the costs, but insisted that they would not make the connection until the house was wired. So we asked the Chora electrician, Adonis, who had saved us from the lethal shower, to wire the house for us. He readily agreed. But each time we made an appointment for him to come to the house, he failed to show up. I would set out on a search and track him down by walking the streets of Chora and asking if anybody had seen him. He would then promise to come the next day—or the following week—and again fail to turn up. It took me weeks to realize that he found it far easier to get me off his back by making an appointment he had no intention of keeping than to admit he had not the faintest idea when he would be free to get on with my work. I finally gave up one day when, the builder having stopped plastering work because he had to wait for the internal wiring to be completed, I traced Adonis to his house. He was in the bath. I asked his wife if I could talk to him because the builders were waiting at the house. She brought back the message that he was committed to his ablutions and that I could look for him the following day.

The Adonis bathing episode was a valuable learning experience and reinforced an impression about Patmian attitudes toward work I had formed from an earlier experience.

This educational episode had occurred when something unspecific had gone wrong with my elderly motorbike and I took it down to the house of Alekos, who knew about such things. I impressed on him the absolute urgency of getting the thing back on the road by Saturday morning, as I needed it for my weekly shop. He assured me there would be no problem.

On Saturday morning I walked down to the house. Alekos was not there. My bike was exactly where I had left it, obviously untouched. I picked my way round to the backyard between eviscerated motorbikes and tins filled with sump oil and chains. Still no sign of him. Then I heard the faint sound of a bouzouki coming from the veranda. I thought at first it was a recording, but the same short passage was being repeated, hesitatingly and with variations. I walked over to the veranda and saw, sitting on the floor, bouzouki across his thighs, an engrossed Alekos. I shouted at him that I needed the bike urgently. I had warned him, I reminded him, and he had told me there would be no problem. He looked up and smiled gently. Yes, but he was sure I would understand. This particular passage on the bouzouki—the fingering was really tricky—he just had to master it before starting work . . .

All I could do was sit and wait until he could play the passage to his satisfaction, at which point he got up, fiddled with the engine and sent me off smartly on my Saturday morning shop. But at least I'd learned something about Patmian priorities.

Agio Pneuma had a timeless atmosphere. We looked out on the sea and the hills. Even the terraces that formed our garden and had been planted with almond trees were craggy with rocky outcrops and bright in the spring with the flowers that covered the mountain slopes outside. We felt so much a part of the mountain that, when urged by friends to protect ourselves from the goats that grazed there by means of a wire mesh fence attached to metal rods sunk in concrete, we could not face the prospect of scarring the mountain, and built a stone wall instead. The lichen-covered rocks that studded the slopes down to the sea would turn from bright yellow at midday to orange brown and glowing red at sunset. They had been there for thousands of years, along with the thorns that spread between them and the crested larks that perched on their peaks. To live in that place felt secure. Things had always been as they were now. They always would be.

One Sunday morning at about six o'clock we were shaken from sleep by a low rumbling on the mountainside. I looked out of the bedroom window and saw a big yellow excavator climbing toward the house. I struggled out of bed and rushed to the wall as the machine stopped, panting and snorting, about six feet away. A head poked out of the window and shouted to me: "I'm sorry. *Petros*. I'm so sorry. *Ekloges*." Then the man lowered the shovel and lumbered toward the timeless rocks. In seconds a cloud of dust hid the excavator as it cut a deep swath across the face of the mountain and pushed the rocks into piles to one side. I was stunned by what was happening, by the speed of the devastation, and puzzled as to the cause. What could *ekloges* possibly mean? Was there oil on the mountain? Since *ekloges* was plural, did it mean a noxious weed that had to be eradicated or a dangerous rodent breeding among the rocks? The yellow color of the excavator meant that it was from the council, so the order for the eradication, if that was what it was, came from the municipal authority. A matter of public health? It had to be something urgently threatening to justify the extent of the destruction.

When the driver paused for a drink, he explained all. (By this time, of course, there was a long leveled patch cut into the face of the mountain, with the rocks piled into a heap at one end of it.) *Ekloges* means "elections," and the race for mayor was about to begin. The serving mayor was not certain of being reelected and so needed a public gesture to win support. The one sure way to be popular on Patmos is to do something for the children. So the mayor had decided to provide them with a playing field by cutting one out of the mountain outside our house.

I protested that we were half a mile from the center of Chora and the children were not going to walk this far out for a game. The driver agreed. I reminded him about the wind, which is always fresh and often strong here, so ball games would be impossible. The driver agreed. But, he pointed out, if anybody comes up with a scheme to help children on Patmos, nobody can criticize it. And people will vote for it.

So a soccer field was cut out, with metal goalposts erected at each end. A few months later, when no soccer enthusiasts had appeared and the place was being used as a dumping ground for builders' rubbish, a wire mesh fence attached to metal rods sunk in concrete was erected around the field. Large metal gates were attached to two concrete posts, with rusty reinforcement rods sticking out of the tops and the names of the builders—ΠΑΝΝΕΛΟΣ, ΛΕΙΠΣΟΙ, ΓΙΝΝΕΛΛΟΣ—deeply scored down the front. Modernity had struck Agio Pneuma.

During the World Cup, four years ago, a bunch of teenagers on motorbikes came to kick a ball around for a few hours, but they soon tired of having to retrieve it when the wind blew it down the mountain. Now the goalposts have fallen and one set has been blown or dragged down the slope. Alexis occasionally shuts his goats inside the wire mesh fence. Vegetation is starting to creep across the barren pitch. The metal gates and concrete posts may last a decade or two, but the mountain is slowly asserting itself. The mayor, by the way, lost the election.

Having failed to get us connected to the Patmos electricity grid because I could not get Adonis out of his bath, I decided to make a virtue of necessity and occupy the moral high ground on the energy question. We went for solar power. This meant that we should not be contributing to the drain on the world's resources of fossil fuels or hastening the collapse of civilization through global warming. Not being technologically adroit, I also took comfort from the fact that it is very difficult to kill yourself with the electricity supplied from a twelve-volt battery.

We bought from Samos a bank of three solar panels, which sat on the roof supported by a metal frame facing due south at an angle of thirty-six degrees. This is the latitude of Patmos, and I read somewhere that the sun would be at that altitude here at midday. So our panels would be best placed for the maximum solar input. They were connected to two industrial twelve-volt batteries like the ones you find in a car, only bigger. I connected the batteries in series and then attached wires to the terminals, which led into the house and powered a series of bulbs like the ones you find in car headlights. We were free from the tyranny of candles, which are charming at a dinner table but hopeless to read by—unless you have a galaxy of them, which makes the room uncomfortably hot. The arrangements were primitive to begin with, but then we had a sudden insight which gave them style.

Most yachts, we thought, were powered by electricity from twelve-volt batteries. But people who had yachts were not notably ascetic; they would not be happy with naked bulbs from a local garage. So we ordered catalogues from yachting suppliers and were delighted and impressed to find a panoply of gadgets that would work within our solar system. There were cabin lights with brass surrounds set in a mahogany base, refrigerators for the cocktail hour, air pumps for inflatable mattresses, kitchen gadgets that shredded and whipped and hi-fi consoles.

The only important service our twelve-volt system could not supply was hot water—heating appliances need more electrical muscle than you can get from batteries. There were, of course, the solar-panel water heaters such as those on the roofs of Scala hotels, but these are designed for heavy consumption, and the two of us would not use enough hot water to keep the system circulating. A friend on Patmos who lives alone had installed one but found that he had to cover the solar panels with a blanket to prevent them from overheating. It seemed perverse to buy solar panels and then have to keep them in the shade, so we tried other methods.

My first attempt at a solution was to paint the tank on the roof with blackboard paint to encourage it to heat up in the sun. But the tank held two cubic meters and even on the hottest day never got beyond lukewarm. Then I had another idea. Every morning the water in the cold tap would run hot for a few seconds, just when you wanted to brush your teeth. This was not the normal cussedness of so-called inanimate matter. It happened because the water had been sitting in a pipe that led from the tank into the house and was in the sun. If I could increase the length of this pipe we would have more hot water. So I bought fifty meters of black plastic garden hose and attached one end to the roof tank. Then I coiled it neatly in a single layer on the roof and attached the other end to the pipe that led to our bathroom. It filled with water from the tank and then sat in the sun all day—and it worked magnificently. I never calculated how much water is in fifty meters of three-quarter-inch pipe, but there was enough for us both to take a shower.

The problem then was that since my system was the only supply of water to the bathroom, we had no cold water there while the sun was up. So we had to time our showers with an eye on the calendar. In April the water was cool enough for teeth brushing before 7 A.M. and hot enough for a shower at around 6 P.M. But by July you could brush teeth only by getting up before 6 A.M., and unless you showered before 10:30 A.M. there was a danger of scalding. The alternative was to wait up for a shower until after 11 P.M., when the water had cooled enough to make it tolerable. If you flushed the loo during the day, the cistern would fill with hot water, which warped the plastic washer and started a serious leak. Unless we heard the trickle, we could lose gallons of precious water down the loo in a matter of hours. So everything that happened in the bathroom was governed by the rotation of the solar system. It may have brought us closer to nature, but it was inconvenient.

Our water supply came from a well in the garden. We called it a well, though wells normally fill themselves with ground-water; ours was just a pit lined with concrete that simply stored the water from the roof during winter rains. We paved the couryard and sloped it so that all rains falling on it would end up in the well, but the dry season on Patmos extends from April to October, and water was scarce at Agio Pneuma.

We stood in a plastic basin when showering, not to save our lives—the twelve-volt system produced no blue flashes—but to save water. Felicia would then dump the daily wash in the basin and jump about on it. Once a week we did the big stuff—sheets and towels—which we had to wring out as a joint effort, grabbing and twisting an end each. It felt like healthy, primitive exercise as we thrashed about dripping and naked; except, of course, that if we had really been primitive there would have been no sheets and towels. The soapy water we then poured onto the plants in the garden. We worried at first about the effect of the soap on growing plants, but when I phoned the BBC Natural History Unit in Bristol, they told me that soap was fine so long as we kept clear of chlorinated detergent.

We borrowed a gas refrigerator, which almost put an end to us. The flame would occasionally blow out in one of the stiff little breezes that curled and eddied around the house and then the gas would seep silently and noxiously into our living space. We would not realize the flame was out until we smelled the gas, because you could only see the flame by lying on the floor and peering under the fridge. I cured this by placing around the flame an ingenious wind shield cut from the lid of a sardine tin, to which was attached a mirror set at an angle so you could see the flame from a standing position. It worked. For three days the flame stayed on; we were able to see it, and the fridge got cold. Unfortunately, however, the kitchen got hot, because it now had in it a gas flame burning twenty-four hours a day. So we handed back the gas fridge and bought a twelve-volt electric one.

We soon discovered that twelve-volt refrigerators are too demanding for a solar panel system—at least the fridge we had, which drained our batteries very quickly. I used to climb onto the roof where the batteries were and test them every morning with a hydrometer, which is a glass tube containing a float to measure the specific gravity of the acid mixture and hence the charge remaining in the batteries. One problem in this procedure was that, because the roof tended to be swept by a brisk breeze, tiny droplets of the acid found their way onto my trousers, which within days looked as though they had been savaged by moths. The outcome of the tests was that three solar panels couldn't cope with a three-cubic-foot refrigerator, not when the daily temperature is in the nineties and the fridge is running day and night. We could have enlarged it, but then the entire roof space would have been taken over by solar panels. Our modest system gave us the choice of either a working fridge with cold water and solid butter during the day, or the possibility of lights in the evenings to read by. We ended up using the fridge on weekends.

I read that more sophisticated systems were able to turn the solar panels through an arc during the day so that they followed the sun at the most productive angle. This seemed an excellent idea, but the technology was beyond me until our son-in-law came for a holiday and fixed the panels to a movable beam with a bolt through one end so that it would swing in a half-circle. By climbing onto the roof every couple of hours during the day and moving the panels, I could manage to keep them at the best angle to the sun and increase the input of power. But the fridge still took it all and asked for more.

An obvious solution to the low input of solar panels was to top up the batteries with wind power. After all, even in Greece, the sun only shines during the day, whereas the wind, especially on a mountaintop, blows day and night. Farther down our mountain slope was a caravan that had attached to it a tower holding aloft the spinning blades of a wind generator. I called on the owner to ask where I could get such a system. He told me it was a waste of time: the output from the generator was so small he had had to buy a set of solar panels, which were far more efficient, to keep his batteries charged; besides which the noise from the whirling blades kept him awake all night. We value our silence at Agio Pneuma, and stayed with the solar panels.

The twelve-volt will not heat up an iron, so clothes go unpressed. There are gas irons, but given our problems with the fridge we decided not to take the risk and went about crumpled. Always adept at rationalization, I decided our creased appearance announced to the world our commitment to saving it from destruction by global warming.

We were encouraged in our self-sufficiency phase by the enthusiasm of the nuns. Noticing that we showed up at church looking as though we had slept in our clothes, and hearing stories of our hauling water in buckets and jumping about on sheets, they would nod their heads slowly, wide-eyed with admiration, and say, "Yes, truly, you are ascetics." This, for a time, went to my head. I happened to be researching the writings of the Desert Fathers for a book on hermits, and so was immersed in the glories of the simple life. My heroes and role models became the men and women who had shunned the comforts of civilization and lived off the land in remote inhospitable regions. They too were crumpled. I could identify with their lifestyle, which seemed to involve sitting around, doing very little all day but plaiting a few leaves and encouraging the odd visiting disciple. The peace and relaxation of a life at one with nature seemed to be within reach.

But I faltered over the diet. Desert Fathers seemed to have one unifying character defect, which was a serious lack of interest in food. They could go for ages without it, and when they troubled to feed themselves at all it was on dry rusks (*paximadia*) and water. We could buy the *paximadia* on Patmos, and I did try one once. It dislodged a filling in an upper molar and tasted of driftwood. As to the water, I had always sympathized with our Russian friends who, if water were brought to the table, would shout for it to be removed, as they were not about to shave. I drank it daily, on the insistence of Felicia, but without enthusiasm.

Felicia had other reasons for loosening our commitment to the ascetic life. She pointed out that washing the clothes by hand, however spiritually uplifting, took hours out of every day; that the long autumn evenings were a problem when we could neither listen to music nor read (the twelve-volt cabin lights were pretty, but not strong enough for prolonged reading without eyestrain). And, that although it might be relaxing to have time off from the comforts of civilization, our lives had so changed that we spent the majority of our hours on Patmos. It followed that we could improve its comfort without endangering our immortal souls.

So we gave way and asked for an extension of the electricity supply. To my surprise, everybody immediately accepted this as a good idea: the local council, the planning authorities and the electricity company. If you have a house on Patmos, it is accepted that you need electricity in the same way you need air and water. We had to pay for the poles, the wires and the work. We had to fill in many forms and wait for many weeks, but nobody challenged our right to a supply. The final problem arose when we discovered that the engineers who would install it paid only brief and unscheduled visits to Patmos. As it happened, they came when we were back in England, but a friend heard they were on the island and waylaid them on our behalf.

In 1996, exactly one hundred and fifteen years after the establishment of the world's first public electricity supply station on Pearl Street, New York, we, at Agio Pneuma, Patmos, were hooked up.

Fourteen

APOCALYPSE REMEMBERED

As 1995 APPROACHED, somebody on Patmos noticed that an anniversary was looming. St. John had been exiled to the island between 94 and 96 A.D., and the accepted date for the writing of the Book of Apocalypse, or Revelation, had been fixed at 95. So plans were laid a year in advance to celebrate the nineteen hundredth anniversary of St. John's vision at the cave. The celebrations seemed likely to split the island into rival factions, each seeking a share of the publicity and its attendant benefits. The central government was going to provide money to help the party go with a swing, and there were many rival claimants for the job of running the show—and for the money that went along with the responsibility.

The Monastery of St. John took first place in the queue. The ecstatic vision of its patron saint was to be celebrated; but the monastery had not been strapped for cash for some time, and there were other bodies involved in the organization of events. The council had a claim to funds: the island had to be groomed into looking its best, and there was talk of the need to import a fire engine and a portable jail for security and public order. The tour operators had the burden of ensuring that the anticipated host of pilgrims and onlookers arrived safely on the island and were properly housed. And since the writing of the Apocalypse can be seen, from one perspective, as a literary and therefore artistic event, there was a mushrooming of arts clubs eager to present exhibitions of paintings, pottery and plays on apocalyptic themes. There was even, we were told, an *Apocalyptic Symphony* in the making, which was to receive its first performance on the island. All of these vied for the attention and the funds of the Ministry of Culture.

Rumor is endemic on Patmos. One is never starved for information, because on a small island, where information is hard to come by, your social status depends not only on who, but on what, you know. So everybody has to claim to know something. This island trait was exploited by the security services when the patriarch made his ceremonial visit on the anniversary of the monastery. It made them redundant. Instead of the itinerary being kept a closely guarded secret, everybody knew its smallest details long before he arrived. His ship, whispered one, would come alongside Scala at 7:22 A.M. precisely. His helicopter, said another, would touch down by the military base at 10 A.M. Others had discovered, and passed on the information in the strictest confidence, that he had been lent a private motor launch by a shipowner and would put in at Grikou at that time. Any would-be assassin would be giddy and exhausted chasing after the unending possibilities. There was no need for a guard.

But in September 1995, we were told world leaders from all the great nations would appear on Patmos. A force of security men one thousand strong was scheduled to arrive before the week of celebration, taking up all available hotel accommodations. The distinguished heads they were to guard were going to have a hard time finding pillows to lay their heads on. The irresistible image rose to our minds of a thousand contented men with sunglasses and earpieces stretching their dark-suited frames on inner-sprung hotel mattresses while their distinguished charges paced the floors of monastic cells to avoid the horror of the straw palliasse.

But asceticism was not obtrusive here in Patmos that apocalyptic September. Indeed, the order went out that every road upon which the patriarchal convoy might possibly travel was to be covered in asphalt, though whether this was to lessen the fatigue of a journey which could take up to twenty minutes or to give an impression of relaxed modernity was unclear. One effect was that the more remote hermitages, which had been built on inaccessible promontories to protect their incumbents from the casual intrusions of the curious, became easily reachable by bicycle, motorbike, taxi or skateboard. Most of the hermits understandably fled. (Any contemporary ascetics who take up residence at one of these hermitages will be comforted by the fact that their sanctuary is now on the home-delivery pizza run.)

Conventions were announced, in which people would come together; and even colloquies, in which people would speak together. It was not made clear what they would be talking about. The Book of Apocalypse has, for nineteen hundred years, successfully resisted all attempts at elucidation, and it seemed unlikely to give up its secrets to the celebrants on Patmos in September 1995.

Nor did it seem that the distinguished visitors were particularly well placed to plumb its depths. Al Gore, the vice president of the United States of America, was not known for his skill in biblical exegesis, and Hillary Clinton was thought to be more concerned with real estate than religion: both were expected. As were the president of France, the chancellor of Germany and the king of Spain. From the world of literary luminaries, we were promised Umberto Eco.

The queen of England was expected to send Prince Philip to represent her, partly because it was rumored that in his declining years he was moving toward the Orthodoxy of his childhood, and partly because of his interest in ecology. This last statement may seem surprising, but it was revealed in the prepublicity of planned events for the Patmos celebrations that the Book of Revelation is, in fact, an ecological tract.

We have, of course, our own island experts on the Apocalypse. I was told here, during the prefestival chats around the tables of our *ouzeries* by those who have given the matter some thought, that St. John saw his visions while he was smoking marijuana—a habit he had taken up to relieve the boredom of exile—and that the Apocalypse was written by his helper, Prochoros (who was quite mad), one morning when St. John had nodded off. These local interpretations have not as yet found their way into the vast academic literature that surrounds the book. I thought they would lend color to the academic colloquies, but in fact the Patmian view was not sought during the event.

Most Patmians were too busy coping with the crowds anyway. All real estate transactions stopped during the summer of 1995, in anticipation of the thousands who were expected to bid against each other for the chance of a place on the island, which had suddenly become the focus of world attention. The tourist season had been slack, but all would be recovered in September when the teeming hordes arrived for the celebrations. We occasionally feel on Patmos, as the tourist season approaches, a close affinity with those other islanders, in the South Pacific, who waited confidently in their cargo cults for the arrival of the great ships bearing treasures from the four corners of the earth.

During the event, only Athenian high society iced our cake. They were led by Prime Minister Andreas Papandreou and his colorful second wife, the former stewardess Mimi, who, it was said, planned to use the Patmos celebrations to lend gravitas to her profile so that she might then launch a political career. These plans were frustrated by the Greek press, which in the days preceding the religious festival published topless photographs of the first lady. Left hanging in the air was the question of how appropriate it might be that she take a leading part in an ecclesiastical proceeding on a Holy Island.

The Papandreous stayed on their yacht and sallied forth from there to gala occasions, not always to happy effect. They arrived, for example, at the most holy moment of an Orthodox liturgy being held outside the cave and proceeded to noisily inspect a nearby guard of honor. The ecumenical patriarch, who was presiding at the liturgy, cannot have been comfortable with the intrusion, and shortly afterwards the Papandreous left without notice. The official explanation issued to the press was that the prime minister had eaten a filet mignon at a local restaurant that disagreed with him. In spite of a hurried denial of this story, issued under threat of litigation by the restaurant, it rapidly became part of Patmos folklore. During the following weeks, members of the opposing political party came on pilgrimage to the restaurant from all over Greece, some to congratulate the chef on almost succeeding in poisoning their political opponent and others to complain that he did a poor job. There was, for a time, a sentimental demand at the restaurant for a dish named Filet Papandreou.

The residents of Patmos, to our mortification and disgust, were ignored during the celebrations. Because the great and the good from all parts of the world were expected and space was limited, tickets were provided only for them and their retinues. At a theatrical extravaganza performed in a newly built outdoor stadium near the cave, crowds of locals pressed against the main gate and were repulsed by security guards while limousines ferried up parties from the Athenian beau monde. We stood sullen and hostile as the shiny suits and glittering gowns chasséd past us, flashing their embossed invitation cards for the television cameras. Tensions were rising and the mood was turning ugly when a local policeman suggested a solution. The one invitation card that had fallen into Patmian hands was recirculated by being passed through the railings, and we all got in.

There was a light and temporary rash of new interpretations of the Book of Apocalypse, but nothing happened, either
on Patmos in 1995 or in the printing presses of Athens later, to
lay bare its secrets. The last book of the New Testament is the
most mystical and poetic of writings. It has been the subject of
countless commentaries; it has inspired sublime works of art; it
has aroused intense religious feelings. But it has also been used
to justify extremism in breakaway cults that are far estranged
from Christianity. It remains one of the most spiritually uplifting and yet potentially dangerous of writings.

Eastern and Western Church attitudes toward the book
have differed from early times. The attitude of the Eastern
Church was that the book was to be treated differently from the
rest of the New Testament. It is not used in the Church's liturgy and is clearly regarded as different in quality from the rest
of the New Testament.

The difference between East and West here seems to be
that the East is more at home with mysticism. In the West there
is a thirst for certainty, for explanation and analysis, which has
led to the many thousands of books that down through the centuries have claimed to reveal the secrets of the apocalyptic text.
One vast and popular class of such works claims to identify historical figures in the book. Usually these have been attempts by
groups of people to assert that their own enemies were God's
enemies. So the book was interpreted by the early Christians as
showing the wrath of God against Nero and the Roman Empire; by the Roman Catholics as against Mohammed and Islam;
by the Protestants as against the pope and the Roman Catho-

lics; and by later generations as against a variety of public enemies such as Napoleon, Hitler and Stalin.

The process continues today. Goods that are sold in the
European Common Market are marked with a bar code, which
is read by computers. There are those who point out that the
Book of Revelation foretells a time when nobody can buy or sell
without the mark of the beast or his number (Revelation 13:17).
The bar code, they say, contains the mark of the beast, and the
European Common Market is a sign that the world is subject
to the reign of the beast.

The identification of the bar code with the mark of the
beast is ingenious. The mark of the beast is 666 (Revelation
13:18). On the bar code there are three pairs of slightly longer
lines that are printed at the beginning, in the middle and at the
end without identifying numbers. The story is that each pair of
longer lines represents the number six and that the failure to
admit this by printing the number is part of the devilish plot.
So we have reached a time when, within the Common Market,
goods that do not bear the mark of the beast may not be sold.
The end is near.

In fact, I am told by computer experts that the three pairs
of slightly longer lines are simply punctuation marks that acti-
vate the reading, indicating the halfway mark and the end of
the bar code. They have no numerical value. When I try here
on Patmos to placate the more strident of the "mark of the beast"
proselytizers with this explanation, I am told that the computer
experts and I are clearly under the spell of the Antichrist.

The disaster at Chernobyl was claimed by many to have
been foretold by the large star that, burning like a torch, fell on

the rivers and springs and turned them bitter so that many died from drinking (Revelation 8:10). The name of the star was Wormwood. When the Chernobyl story was in the headlines, the Western press announced with a flourish that the English word "wormwood" translates into the Russian word *chernobyl*. Here, the papers claimed, we have an unambiguous prophecy that foretells the present disasters to our world, clearly documented. Now, in fact, Russian encyclopaedias make it clear that *chernobyl* refers to *Artemisia vulgaris*, which is mugwort, not *Artemisia absinthium*, which is wormwood. And the reference in the Apocalypse is not a prophecy of future disaster but an echo of the Old Testament record of God's turning the waters of a rebellious people bitter by using wormwood (Jeremiah 9:13 and 23:15). Like so much apocalyptic literature, the Book of Revelation was written for contemporary readers and not for excitable futurists two thousand years later.

But millenarians plague Patmos. Those who believe that the Book of Revelation contains clues that foretell the end of the world are often keen to spend time on the island where the book was written, perhaps to increase their chances of being among the blessed on the latter day. They seem to overlook the very clear specifications at the beginning of chapter 14: that the only people to be saved will be 144,000 male virgins who have learned a new song that nobody else can learn. These qualifications clearly rule out most of the people who have approached me with shining eyes and the message that they are saved.

Fifteen

☞ A Place of Healing . . .

I BEGAN THIS book by spitting at the devil and wondering if I might be slightly unhinged. After twelve years spent mostly on Patmos as an apprentice Christian, my perspectives have changed. The world seems to me a different place now, and I should, perhaps, talk about that. To say something of how the world appears from Patmos is to disclose something about Patmos itself, for we are most revealing about ourselves when we talk about other people.

To get the devil out of the way—Orthodoxy teaches us not to waste time on him—it now seems to me unwise to discount the presence of evil in the world. When I read that an army in Africa is rounding up two-year-old children and cutting off their hands, I cannot put this down to revolutionary zeal, political commitment or economic need. It seems to me quite simply evil. Any other explanation is contrived.

It would be depressing to haul out of the headlines other evidence of the existence of evil. It is there to be seen and, certainly from Patmos, it is easily recognized. What seems curious from here is that so much of the rest of the civilized world has rejected the reality of evil and is committed to the view that all human aberrations can be explained away by psychotherapists: that we only do wrong if we are warped by broken relationships, a deprived childhood or low self-esteem. But then, a force of evil can operate most effectively when people have convinced themselves it does not exist. I am not convinced.

Something strange seems to have happened in the world outside to the spirit of tolerance and liberalism. Once they were rightly thought to be high ideals for all societies. But we now have a situation in which cultures are esteemed not for the lofty ideals to which they aspire but for their readiness to put up with less than lofty practices. People are judged for being judgmental; to exercise discrimination is illiberal; to suggest that human beings have different levels of ability is to be labeled a fascist.

On a lighter note, about once a week I get a letter of congratulations from some company I have never heard of. It announces with a blare of large print that I have come triumphantly through a series of complicated and difficult tests. Thousands of other names have been weeded out and my name alone stands clearly in front and ready to be submitted for the final screening. This will happen soon and could result in my winning a luxury car, a world cruise or, most depressing of all, a visit to my home by a cheery group with colored balloons, a television camera and an outsize check made out in my name for an enormous sum. All I have to do is agree to buy something I don't want. From the perspective of Patmos, I have to wonder: does there really exist out there a credulous group of people so numerous as to make the expense of these ridiculous campaigns worthwhile? The market researchers must have discovered they are there.

It is something of a cliché to suggest that the world outside is preoccupied with getting and spending. We have to put a lot of time and energy into those activities here on the island. I think the difference is that it would not occur to us to think of such activities as the main, let alone the sole, reason for our existence.

WE ARE NOT TOTALLY NAIVE. The Greek admiration for the trickster is deeply rooted in classical history. It goes right back to the *Iliad,* when Nestor, the famous charioteer, advises his son on how to win a race. The cunning man using the right tactics, he points out, can come in first even with second-rate horses. A man with craft is called a *poniros,* which means a rogue or knave who gets on by bending the rules. When we talk about him today, we shake our heads and smile. Most Greeks, it must be admitted, would prefer their political leaders, their investment advisers and especially their accountants to have a touch of the *poniros.* It would show a culpable want of prudence to place one's financial affairs in the hands of someone wholly without guile.

But, although we may give the *poniros* his due in human activities, we regularly pray to escape his clutches. In the phrase "deliver us from evil" of the Lord's Prayer, the word "evil" is a translation of *poniros*. And a world in which the *poniros* is unreservedly admired and unfailingly successful is seen on Patmos as a fallen one. We may have to live in it, to go along with it, even to adopt its ways; but we occasionally have nostalgia for a time that never was but ought to be, in which nice guys don't finish last.

In fact, "nice guys" on Patmos—and the phrase, of course, includes both sexes—are recognized by everyone and even labeled as such. They have a quality that is called *charis*. The dictionary defines the word as "charm" or "grace." It does exist elsewhere, but rarely. Here on the island you might find it in the baker, the dustman, a priest, a schoolteacher—I have seen it in all of them—and you recognize it immediately. It shows first in the eyes. They are calm, steady, mild, full of interest but without aggression. The person with *charis* has humility in the sense that the Desert Fathers understood it: not as an ingratiating meekness but as a keen interest in and enthusiasm for the other person. It has to be admitted that sometimes people with *charis* do come in last. But that is not a law of our society.

On Patmos, those who have finished first are respected for not flaunting it. I was having a drink one evening with Vangelis outside his restaurant when he pointed out one of a circle of seemingly identical old men sipping ouzo at a table across the square. They were all in their seventies, grizzled, bespectacled and wearing clothes that had been bought many years before at a local store. They might have been old boys of the local school getting together for a nightly ritual reminiscence of shared experiences. Except that the one Vangelis pointed out had been abroad, built up a great fortune and returned to Patmos to make generous donations to public projects. He still caught the ten o'clock bus down to Scala every morning to do his shopping. There is something healthy in a society that notices and esteems such people.

Of course, Patmos is changing. A Patmian friend, Jiannis, told me recently that he had invited a friend to a wedding one morning in August. Weddings are important on Patmos. Jiannis had known his friend for over thirty years. Friendship is important on Patmos. The friend looked serious and shook his head. He could not attend the wedding. August is when the tourists are here. "You understand," he said. "August is money time." Jiannis understood, and was saddened by the change. An important shift of priorities had taken place in his lifetime.

TELEVISION HAS STARTED its grim work of distraction. The Greeks have a pungent word to describe its effects: *psychofthoros*—"that which rots the soul." But the most obvious effects are in fashion. The most popular TV shows on Patmos, as elsewhere in the less developed world, are Hollywood soaps such as *Dallas* and *Santa Barbara*. One consequence of this is that the young women of Patmos totter along the streets on precipitously high heels, wearing broad padded shoulders and strung about with yards of brass chains; their men strut stiffly in crotch-crushing jeans held up by broad-buckled cowboy belts, instead of the easy floppy cotton trousers their fathers wore.

IT SEEMS HERE that the Western civilization that sends us newspapers and television programs is preoccupied with inessentials.

Over there, reality is the sum total of everything that impinges on the senses, which can be seen, touched, weighed and measured. Of most immediate concern are the things that can be bought and sold.

A tiny minority of the population over there—about 2 percent in Britain—regularly takes time off once a week on a Sunday morning to concern itself with spiritual matters in church. Some of these have a real commitment to Christian faith. The rest of the population either totally ignores the supernatural or tinkers with it in the spirit it brings to computer games. So astrology flickers improbably on and star columns persist in newspapers; you can buy crystals to focus your inner energies and essential oils to pacify your inner self; meditation mats and joss sticks keep on selling; even religion itself can be occasionally trendy, so long as those who teach it are agreeably exotic. Hindu gurus and Buddhist lamas attract the educated classes of Europe and America, who are strangers to the faith of their own culture. It used to be said that black people have a natural sense of rhythm; now it seems that brown people are closer to God.

The main attraction of these Eastern religions is that they chime in with today's passion for self-realization. By locating God not on a judgment throne above but in the hearts of believers, they at once sweep away a stern morality and encourage self-absorption. It is much more agreeable to be told that the Supreme Being is not at a distant celestial vantage point recording our misdeeds, but rather lying curled up deep inside each one of us, waiting to be discovered.

What seems to me strange here on Patmos, the island of St. John, is that the West seems to have forgotten that precisely this Eastern religious teaching is at the heart of his gospel, which is itself at the heart of Christianity. The Orthodox Church has preserved and still teaches that the final goal of all Christians is the awakening of the divine that lies within us, a process which it calls "deification." This is what St. Peter clearly sets out as the promise of Christ, that we may escape the corruptions of the world and "become partakers of the divine nature" (2 Peter 1:4). So we do not need to turn to India or Tibet to learn this. It is at the very foundation of the traditional faith of our own culture.

Also from St. John we learn to respect the faiths of other lands. The Logos was there from the beginning, before the incarnation of Christ. So the religious insights of the great faiths of the East are not to be despised as in conflict with Christianity but to be respected as valid in themselves and shining a light that even today can penetrate the darkness of the post-Christian West.

I BEGAN BY DESCRIBING PATMOS as a place of power. It still draws to its shores a far-flung group of regular visitors, many of whom have been coming to the island every summer for twenty or thirty years. They do not own property here; they stay always in rented rooms or the older hotels. They know Patmos well, as they do many of its people. Many of them speak Greek and have formed long friendships with families on the island. Patmos has become an indispensable part of their lives, and they fall naturally into its ways and rhythms as soon as they arrive, even though their home environments are very different. We have good friends among these long-distance commuters from Milan,

Johannesburg, Zurich and Philadelphia. These are the most interesting people to talk to about the special qualities of Patmos, because they make the decision to travel long distances and come here every year. I have spent many hours asking them about the qualities of Patmos that draw them here in the hope of better understanding those qualities myself.

THERE IS GENERAL AGREEMENT on three points. The first one is that Patmos is unique—many of the people I've talked to have traveled widely in the Greek islands, and some have tried to form a relationship with other places, but they have always come back to Patmos. Second, the special quality of Patmos is spiritual. This has nothing to do with St. John, since most of the people who come here are not even nominally Christian. Rather, it is the awareness on the island of a dimension not evident elsewhere. The third point of agreement is that this unique spiritual dimension of the island is at the same time powerful and ineffable. So there is no point in my trying to describe it in words.

A French philosopher told me that on his first visit to Patmos he felt strongly that he was "somewhere." There are so many places, he explained, which don't give you the feeling that you are anywhere in particular; but on Patmos, he and I agreed, you are certainly somewhere.

I discussed the attraction of Patmos with someone who runs a bookshop in Zurich and has been returning here annually for over twenty years. She said its appeal was that it is a place of bare essentials. The landscape is one of rocks and hills, with few trees—indeed with so little vegetation that you get the feeling that everything you see is as it has always been. In the city everything around you is man-made and will not be around for long. On Patmos the things that surround you are natural and have a feeling of eternity. In the city it is also hard to distinguish between necessities and luxuries, especially as there is so much pressure on everybody to feel they can't live without some product or other. On Patmos there is the opportunity to reassess priorities.

The annual visit to Patmos is a chance to take a look at yourself, free from the distractions of life in the city. The experience changes you for a time, and when you leave the island you keep something of Patmos inside you.

In contrast, there are those who come to Patmos, especially at the height of the summer, for a different sort of experience. I heard about it from a French civil servant who has been coming here for ten years. His daily ritual begins around midday when he crawls out of bed for his first coffee. He lies on the beach until about 5 P.M., when it's time for breakfast. After that, it's another coffee and a smoke in a waterfront café for a couple of hours before heading back to a rented room for a shower and change. Then the first ouzo in another café—for a change of scenery and for company. He dines at about 10:30 P.M. and afterward goes to a nightclub in Chora as the excitement of the evening kicks off. There he drinks whiskey with diligence until about 2 A.M., when the bar closes. Then he goes down to a bar in Scala which stays open till 4 A.M., after which he staggers back to his room.

In Paris, where this man lives and works, he is a nonsmoker and a moderate drinker. On Patmos he goes through three packs of cigarettes and a bottle of whiskey a day. He feels physically terrible but spiritually elated. He tells me there are dozens of people who follow this routine. I don't have the stamina to check up. But they are, I suppose, all striking out in search of something different, and maybe discovering spirituality by a different path. And Patmos caters to many different people on the many different paths that lead up the mountain.

An incident that happened to me some years ago made me realize the special insight Patmos can give. The day had begun badly when Felicia and I quarreled. I don't remember why; it was nothing serious, but it opened a gulf between us that hurt. I went off down the mountain in my cowardly way to escape the tensions of home and found myself walking in the valley of Kipos, which lies between our house and the sea. To the left of the path was a flat field covered in flowers, all planted in rows and carefully tended. At the other side of the field was the stone cottage of our friend Vassos, who takes away the village rubbish with his string of donkeys. I had a sudden idea that if I could arrive back at home with an armful of flowers I might be in a good position to heal a rift.

So I walked around the edge of the field to the little courtyard outside Vassos's cottage, where he was sitting at the door making some repairs to a wooden saddle. We greeted each other and talked about the weather and our health and the health of our wives and children. After satisfying the demands of local etiquette—that any visit to anybody must seem to be spontaneous and to have no purpose—I asked if I might take a few of his flowers back to the house.

Vassos nodded and strode off between the rows of flowers, picking to the left and right until he had an armful, which he thrust at me. I reached for my wallet and asked, "How much do I owe you?"

"Owe me? For what?"

"For the flowers?"

"The flowers? How much what?"

I was getting worried. Vassos was not a dull man, and perhaps my Greek was letting me down again. I waved my wallet at him.

"How much *money?*"

There was a pause. His eyebrows came together, and then they shot upward in sudden comprehension.

"You mean—*money?* For—*flowers?*"

He looked at me as if I had just arrived from another planet.

"Flowers are beauty," he said. "They are from God. They *are* God." He paused and shook his head. "You cannot exchange flowers for"—his nose wrinkled with distaste—"for *money.*"

I felt reprimanded, but puzzled. "What about all these flowers?" I asked, pointing to the neat rows of blossoms, clean and weeded and arranged like a professional nurseryman's fields back home. "All this means a lot of work—planting and weeding and watering every day . . . surely—"

"For the churches," he interrupted. "They are to bring beauty to the churches. And there are many churches on Patmos."

He filled my arms with flowers and patted my shoulder. As I left I could hear him chuckling to himself: *Money! For flowers!!*"

We do not know, here on Patmos, what God is. We are sometimes awakened to His existence through becoming aware of His energies. The quite unnecessary beauty of flowers is an expression of those energies. Flowers are a particular mode of God's self-disclosure, a divine reality that expresses itself as . . . flowers. Yes, flowers are God.

AT THE END OF CHAPTER 9 I described the marble plaque which the monks of Patmos set into the wall of their library shortly after Edward Clarke had removed some of their most precious books. It gave to the library the beautiful name of "A Place of Healing for the Soul." To those who have come to love Patmos, who have felt its power and experienced its unique qualities, there can be no better description of the island.